Personal Meaning

Personal Meaning

How We Give Relational Significance, Relative Importance, Emotional Force, and Moral Value to Our Actions

RICHARD PRUST

Cover painting entitled *True Romantic* is used by permission of the artist, Jeffery Geller.

Published by State University of New York Press, Albany

© 2026 State University of New York

EU GPSR Authorised Representative:
Logos Europe, 9 rue Nicolas Poussin, 17000, La Rochelle, France
contact@logoseurope.eu

For information, contact State University of New York Press, Albany, NY
www.sunypress.edu

Library of Congress Cataloging-in-Publication Data

Name: Prust, Richard C. (Richard Charles), 1939– author.
Title: Personal meaning : how we give individual and relational significance, relative importance, emotional force, and moral value to our actions / Richard Prust.
Description: Albany : State University of New York Press, [2026]. | Series: SUNY series in American philosophy and cultural thought | Includes bibliographical references and index.
Identifiers: ISBN 9798855806021 (hardcover : alk. paper) | ISBN 9798855806045 (PDF) | ISBN 9798855807189 (epub)
Subjects: LCSH: Respect for persons. | Personalism. | Self-consciousness (Awareness).
Classification: LCC BJ1533.R42 P784 2026
LC record available at https://lccn.loc.gov/2025034941

Contents

Acknowledgments

I am especially grateful to Bill Throop, Gordon Whitaker, Doug Kelly, Keith Gribble, and Readers "A" and "B" of SUNY Press: All of you worked with drafts as the book progressed, and all of you made numerous suggestions that improved it. And thanks to you for the cover art, Jeffery Geller, my old friend and collaborator on an earlier book.

Introduction

All of us watch and listen to other people. We assume that what they do and say has meaning for them and that we can often discern that meaning by grasping their intent. On that basis, we professionally characterize their actions, as psychologists, lawyers, demographers, anthropologists, counselors, actors, and detectives. In our off hours, we grasp what people are doing nonprofessionally: "She's picking the kids up from school." "He's renewing his driver's license." "The lawyers are trying to stall."

My interest in this book is with two distinct ways we characterize people's actions, personal and impersonal. As I use the terms, an impersonal characterization of action is one that designates it as a *kind* of action: "He got off the elevator on the third floor." "She bought 100 shares of Amalgamated Paperclip." "He always drinks coffee with breakfast." Getting off the elevator, buying shares of stock, and drinking coffee with breakfast are kinds of things people do. Specifying actions by their kind is immensely useful, particularly in the social and behavioral sciences. It allows us to correlate specimens of active behavior, report on them, and reason about them in ways we think of as objective and factual.

These same actions, however, meant something more to the person who did them than to any objective observer. For the actor, they had a *personal* meaning. This too is meaning we can reason about. It is relevant, for example, to most moral or legal judgments. Setting the fire was an act of arson, not an accident, and paying for a Supreme Court justice's holiday was a bribe, not just a friendly gesture: These are judgments we have reason for making.

Whether we characterize actions from a personal or an impersonal perspective depends on the kind of reasoning appropriate to the judgments we want to make. That may seem obvious, and it is, but what I think gets underappreciated by many who reason about what people do is the distinctive set of rules in play when our reasoning concerns the personal meaning of their action. Raising our awareness of those patterns of inference—of their logic, if you will—is foundational for my objectives in this book. We are going to see that by tracing that logic, we can clarify our thinking about a wide variety of topics, particularly those listed in the book's subtitle.

One difference seems evident from the start. The meaning an action has for its actor tends to be richer and more nuanced than its meaning for a casual observer. The bride's words "I do" have a richer, more nuanced meaning for her than they do in the ears of a witness in the back row. He sees only the simple fact that she is taking the vow.

The richness and nuance derive from something distinctive about human agency, namely that it is multi-intentioned. It is this fact about our agency—that at any one time we have multiple intentions—that serves as the founding premise for this account. We also take as a given that we often find ourself in the process of advancing more than one intention in what we are doing, a fact made evident by *how* we are doing what we are doing. That is because, being multi-intentioned, we are most fully actualized when we coordinate our multiple concurrent intended achievements. The *personal* meaning of our action, as we will come to understand it, is the context of meaning determined by how we are coordinating our active life at the time. In ways we will investigate, its personal meaning is determined in part by how we make it fit into that coordination. What I hope to demonstrate is that, by appreciating how we characterize our actions as components of a coordinated life, we can clarify the logic of our appraisals of their relational significance, their relative importance, their emotional force, and their moral value.

We are going to see in the chapters ahead how confusing it can be in all these matters when we confine ourselves to reasoning impersonally. Our first step toward addressing the confusions will be to contrast personal and impersonal reasoning. This will require a certain amount of codifying the inferences we commonly draw about personally meaningful actions and contrasting that scheme with the logic we use when we reason with categories or kinds of action.

We start with some features of the basic vocabulary we use in this agentive universe of discourse. There, we talk about what someone's "intention" was, what they "meant" to be doing, and what the "character" of their action was as they saw it. Often we use these terms as equivalents.

We say that if someone intends to do something, they mean to do it, and that what they mean to do, they intend to do. To give meaning to an action is to characterize it, so what we intend or mean to be doing is action of a certain character, and our action has that character and can be so characterized.

The correlation between an act having character, being intentional, and being meant reveals something about actions that makes them formally distinct from mere behavior. Both acting and behaving involve movement, but we see someone's movement as action only if we assume that they are aware of moving that way and that they mean to be doing so. Just now, for instance, I assume that you are not only aware of reading these sentences but that you mean to be doing so.

Another feature of the personal meaning of our action is that we are typically in a better position to discern its personal character than are those who might observe us. Friends may know us well, but usually not as well as we know ourself. Here, too, we can imagine someone saying, "You know me better than I know myself," and we find it reasonable to believe that Sigmund Freud was able to identify intentions in his patients' actions that they were in the dark about. As a rule, though, we give most people credit for knowing their intentions better than others do.

The reason we usually know our own intentions better than outsiders do has to do with that complexity of our intentional life that I mentioned earlier. If you, someone I do not know personally, were to peer through the window and see me just now thumping away at the computer keyboard, you would correctly characterize what I was doing as typing (notice: a type of action). I too am also actively aware of typing. But I am also aware of starting a book and trying to get clear about some ideas I have been toying with for decades. And you, just now reading these sentences, are aware of reading them, but perhaps you are also aware of weighing whether to read further, or assessing whether they merit publication, or reading them before bed because they unfailingly put you to sleep. Such intentions are also what you mean to be doing.

This points to the fault line separating the logics of personal and impersonal meaning. The multiple elements of our intentional life complicate the meaning of our action in ways that put it beyond the grasp of any *kind* of action. Suppose A gives B a gift. A would agree that this category of action, "gave a gift," accurately describes what he did. But as to what he meant to be doing, there was more to it. It turns out that A also meant to demonstrate his fondness for B. He also meant to ingratiate himself with

B's family for business reasons. Truth be told, in giving such an expensive gift he also meant to convey the impression that he was wealthy. All these intentions were factors in what he meant to be doing. For that reason, the kind of action we call "gift giving" is correct but inadequate to convey the *personal* intention/meaning/character of his gift giving.

At this point, if you are a student of human action who reasons using categories, you may suspect me of being naive to the possibilities of your method. You might claim to represent the personal meaning of A's action by conjoining accurate characterizations of each of A's multiple intentions. The personal significance of A's gift giving would simply be a conjunction of "giving B a gift," "trying to ingratiate himself," "trying to convey the impression. . . ," and whatever other intentions he may have had. You might point to the success of various commercial enterprises that compound someone's intentions to gain a sufficient working approximation of the personal meaning of purchases they are likely to make. It suffices, for instance, for digital advertising. All those little categories of action revealed by our browsing habits contribute to an algorithmic ID for ad placement. For that and many other purposes, you might insist that our personal life is sufficiently disclosed by conjoining the categories of action revealed by our browsing.

But for our purposes in this book—to understand how the meaning of our action can have relational significance, relative importance, emotional force, and moral value—a conjunction of intentions cannot suffice. Something crucial about our intentional life eludes the grasp of any compilation of its agenda items. Here is the difference: Compilation can grasp the individual intentions motivating A, but it cannot grasp how A is *coordinating* the achievement of those intentions. It can prehend the various things A is doing, but it cannot comprehend them as meaningful action. We do not have to monitor our active awareness for long to see how routinely and frequently we revise the character of what we are doing to *coordinate* it with some other element of our life. The way we draw it into coordination modifies its meaning for us, and, once modified, its meaning cannot be categorized. Hence the need for an alternative logic of characterization.

To distinguish impersonal from personal logic in a preliminary way, let me contrast it with the basic formal features of category logic, the logic many of us learned in Logic 101. As Aristotle formalized it millennia ago, reasoning about factual claims requires us to think of them as claims about category membership. "All men are mortal" makes the claim that all the beings we categorize as "men" can also be categorized as "mortal." The presumption is that if we represent statements as claims about category inclusion and exclusion, we make possible a process of reasoning—constructing syllogisms—that can draw any reasonable inference among propositions on any topic.

Aristotle did not invent reasoning with categories; he discovered it. Category logic was operational before he codified it, as readers of Plato's dialogues can attest. But by displaying how it works, he made us more aware of what supports our sense of validity when we follow it.

The alternative reasoning we will explore here is what I call "character logic." It is the reasoning we do when we characterize actions according to how they are coordinated in someone's life. To grasp the difference, we need not invent some system with novel notations like the ones symbolic logicians employ. We can make ourself aware of character logic just by paying close attention to how we deliberate our options before making important decisions, or how we characterize someone's intentions when we decide whether or not to trust them. By tracing many such inferences, we can discern the rules we follow, and by making them explicit we disclose character logic. Though it sounds presumptuous to say, while I did not invent character logic—indeed, it seems to be more primitive than reasoning with categories—I do propose to codify it, at least enough to account for what validates the health of our personal relationships, the validity of our decisions about relative importance, our justification for feeling the emotions we feel, and our discernment of the moral value of what we do.

We began by observing that personal meaning is distinctive in that it is informed by multiple intentions, like A's gift giving. In formal terms, this assumes that human agency can be *multi-intentioned* in a single moment. We may not be the only animals who do more than one thing at a time, but our linguistic skills give us the means to coordinate our achievement of many more concurrent projects than dolphins, chimps, and other clever animals can. It is something that makes human agency distinctive.

Imagine a person—call her Jill—who leads a normally complex adult life. By calling her multi-intentioned, I mean simply that there are multiple courses of action she would agree she is presently advancing. She could, if asked, say "yes" to questions like: "Oh, are you leaving the party so soon?" "Are you still paying off your student loan?" "Are you seeing anyone these days?" "Are you still reading that Iris Murdoch novel?," and "Are you planning any travel this summer?" These are all questions about

Jill's present intentional life: At present, she projects each of them toward completion over some span of time. But she imagines each with its own time scheme. Some are projected toward completion in the near term, like the novel reading. Others are indefinitely ongoing, like the relationship. Some are in their inception, like leaving the party. Some are long-term, like paying off the loan. Some are projected for the future, like summer travel. But—and this is key—all can be said to be determining how she *currently* projects her life into the future.

As I insisted earlier, Jill is more than the sum of her namable intentions, which is why we expect mature people like Jill to be achieving her agenda items in a coordinated way. Why so? Because coordinating her achievements is *mandated by her nature as a multi-intentioned agent.* The character logical connection is simple: For Jill to actualize herself as an agent is, by definition, for her to achieve her intentions. Given that she is a human agent, she actualizes herself more by achieving more of what she intends. It follows that the more she is achieving, the more fully actualized she is.[1] There is one tried and true way for Jill to perform optimally. She must actualize as much of her intentional life as she can by coordinating it as best she can. We can conclude that the practice of personal self-actualization requires an ongoing intention to coordinate her life as well as she can.

This argument—that our very nature as a multi-intentioned agent requires us to achieve our agenda as fully as we can by coordinating it—establishes what I will call our "personal imperative." If to be is to act, and if achieving as much of our agenda as possible is what most fully actualizes us, we are obliged to coordinate our life as well as we can. It is an imperative we cannot ignore without failing to be who we intend to be.

Of course, Jill is "only human" as well as "distinctively human." She is bound at times to get her intentions tangled and find herself on (or over) the edge of doing something jeopardizing the success of her other projects. For instance, one spring she planned a summer trip without budgeting for car payments; another time she got so immersed in watching pet videos that dinner burned on the stove. Happily, such times are rare and she chides herself when they arise. Early in adolescence, she learned that setbacks, frustrations, and disappointments will be her lot if she does not project her actions in mutually accommodating ways.

I suggested earlier that the rolling accommodations we practice in ordinary life continually modify how we mean/intend/characterize our actions. The way we do so makes what we do *personal* in meaning. For example:

Today finds Jill doing the weekly housecleaning. Ordinarily the job takes little concentration, so she mostly gives her active attention to planning, pondering, and daydreaming. But not today. Her mother will soon arrive for a visit, and she is determined to impress her with a meticulously cleaned apartment.

As a formal matter, we can say about Jill's intentional life that she presently intends both to clean the apartment and to impress her mother. Both projects presently characterize her active life. They are both on her agenda. A nosy neighbor could see that she is cleaning the apartment, but that would be the extent of it. Jill is aware of doing both things. She manifests her awareness of trying to impress her mother in how she cleans—exerting herself more, moving more furniture, and dusting more shelves.

The imaginative feat Jill is achieving—that of projecting two or more intended achievements in one course of action—is the most basic skill she uses in coordinating her intentional life. It is going to figure prominently in our account, so let us call it by an appropriate name. Jill, we will say, is "resolving" two intentions by modifying how she does one to accommodate the other. I think you will agree that much of our active life is steered by resolving in this sense. It is how we coordinate what we do with other elements of our intentional life. Though I use the word "resolve" as a term of art by formulating it this way, it does seem to square nicely with common usage. If we asked Jill why she is cleaning in such a determined and thorough way, it would make sense for her to say that she is resolved to show a clean apartment to her mother. That usage also squares with our recognition that people can be highly resolved in doing some things and not very resolved in doing others. If someone is highly resolved in some endeavor, say running for mayor, we would assume that she is leading much of her life in ways supportive of her campaign. On the other hand, if someone stumbled upon a TV show and it piqued his interest, we would not see him as resolved to watch it. After a time, if he found himself so engaged with it that he postponed dinner, it would be reasonable to say that he seemed resolved to watch it.

We also follow common usage in calling such episodes of modifying a projected course of action "moments of resolve." Each such moment accommodates something we are doing to bring it into better accord with something else we are doing. Think of some of the different situations when we find ourself doing this. Sometimes we face a conflict between two things we mean to do, and we resolve our intentions to remove the conflict. Other times we seize on the possibility of synergizing elements of our life by projecting them anew. Conflict resolution is called for when the way we have been intending to do something threatens to impinge on some other element of our intentional life; synergizing resolutions are called for when we can imagine advancing some other element of our life more successfully if we modified something we are doing now.

Of course, moments of resolve only occur when our agentive needs call for it. Most of the time we move along our intended paths of achievement without having to negotiate conflicts and without being seized by novel opportunities. But even the most settled among us must from time to time resolve the course of our action anew. If, as we are assuming, to act is to mean/intend/characterize some achievement, and if achieving multiple intentions efficiently requires resolving them in reimagined courses, then the succession of those moments of resolve would intend to sustain individuality through continually coordinating our agency. In other words, the structure of our agency militates in favor of normative continuity of character, the identity of which we deem to be that of an individual person. All of this happens, or at least tends to happen, because the requirements of success as a multi-intentioned agent require it. The need to imagine new projections of resolve are prompted by constant fluctuations in our shape-shifting place in the world. We create and recreate continuity among our actions over time, and if enough of our intentional life is included in that continuity, we become justified in thinking of ourself as *a single course of action* bearing individual personal identity *as that projected course.*

The Chapters Ahead

Chapter one describes how we coordinate our life well enough to establish our agency as personal. It investigates how successive recalibrations in the moments of our resolve foster our sense of overall coordination. We will also explore why our awareness of the way we are coordinated prevents us from attending to ourself as a whole. Because it is tacit, we cannot objectify it in our awareness. It is, however, possible to describe how we are aware of being a person without objectifying it. We will find that we are tacitly aware of it in a way akin to how we are tacitly aware of the arc of a storyline in the novel we are reading. We are aware of *who* we are as a narrative arc contextualizing our present action.

The analogy we need to explore—and the limits of that analogy—is between how a person is resolved in acting and how a story is resolved in its telling. The analogy is powerful and it will be crucial for understanding personal meaning, but we must also highlight and keep in mind certain features that make it unlike conventional narrative resolve.

The functional distinctiveness of personal resolve is one that we have already observed: we try to resolve our lives to achieve more of what we intend. Form follows function. Moreover, to integrate a complex intentional life narratively, we must use a distinctive temporal logic. Conventional stories are told entirely in the past tense. They give narrative significance only to moments of completed actions. Personal stories project action into the future as well. They give narrative significance to the past and future of the resolve we presently project. In any active moment, we project our life as the context for what we are then resolved to achieve. That way, we make ourself the protagonist of a storylike imaginative projection contextualizing the present moment in a coherent course that identifies both past and future moments of action.

If chapter 1 succeeds in describing a form of narrative imagination that functions to integrate our intentional life well enough to make us identifiable to ourself as an individual, we will enjoy some philosophical payoffs. For one thing, we will find ourself able to avoid the "which-came-first" puzzle—the one that asks whether the person gives rise to the character of their actions or their actions give rise to their identity as a person. If a person is both the creator and subject of their narrative, both are true. Their personal story gives them character as an individual—in that sense, identifies *who* they are—*and*, in that as a multi-intentioned agent they are advancing it by intentionally modifying their course of coordinated actions, they are the continuing author of their identity. My story authorizes me in that the resolution it achieves gives me coherence and identity as an individual personal being; I, as a multi-intentioned agent, authorize my story by projecting it to coordinate my present life optimally.

In outline, the first chapter argues that

- To be an agent is to achieve intentionally.

- As a multi-intentioned agent, we are achieving in multiple ways at any one time.

- Since our multi-intentioned agency is best actualized in accomplishing as many of our intentions as we can, the better we coordinate them, the more actualized we are, and the more actualized we are, the more we are who we project ourself to be.

- Thus, we are prompted by the very form of our agency to coordinate as much of our intentional life as we can. This is our personal imperative.

- The narrative projection governing our life has legitimacy as our personal story by virtue of actualizing us best.

- That story contextualizes the meaning of our action so as to make it personal; in advancing it, we are personally present in the character of what we do.

Chapter 2 explores how at least some of our actions bear relational significance. Not all do. In brushing my teeth or searching a website, I am coordinating only my own movements. But when we interact—consult with a pharmacist, sing a duet, have a dinner conversation—the character of what we do is not exclusively ours to determine. We are aware of collaborating on a project that involves coordinating our movements with another's. The way interactive coordination is achieved is instructive for understanding our relational life, and we can do that best, I think, by comparing its form to that of our individual achievements.

The analogy between resolving our own movements and coordinating them interactively is based on the fact that both activities involve shared intentions. When we act as an individual, the intention common to our movements is what coordinates those movements. The movements share a single intention. The same holds true for interactions. Every successful interaction is steered both by the discrete aims of the interactors and by an intention they share to coordinate the achievement of those individual aims. A shared intention gives both grace to our individual achievements and health to our interactivity.

Notice how the personal imperative prompts us to be interactive in many of our undertakings. It prompts us to interact when it is agentively advantageous—we get more done—and to withdraw when it is not. We need to determine in each case whether sharing an intention with this person promises to enhance us. Sharing intentions interactively can open a way to enlarge the scope of movement we determine in character by our resolve, which is a formal way of saying that it increases who we are. Just as resolving our individual actions makes possible intending a greater body of movement, so too interacting successfully allows us to project the greater body of movement we mutually intend, thus enlarging us by the range of movement actualized collaboratively by the character of our resolve. That is the fundamental reason—if you will, the ontological reason—for our personal disposition toward social and communal lives: Healthy interactions—those intended by both parties to serve both parties' interests—promise greater actualization to the parties to them.

There is this to be kept in mind, however. The personal imperative is addressed to individuals. It draws up its mandate with respect to a specific active life executed with a specific physical body, our body, the one we are the life of. Nonetheless, in interacting and coming to share the characterization of a joint body of movement interactively, the field of achievement we are resolved upon includes more than our own movements.

It is interesting to notice how this bit of common sense—that we can be part of each other's lives—gets glossed over by the standard mind--indexed or body-indexed models of personal identity. In identifying a person as a character of resolve, we justify our intuitive sense of sharing active lives. In moments of interaction, we are aware of moving in an expanded field of movement, an achievement the character of which we jointly determine. As we will see, this is even more the case when the interaction is personal. Then we are aware of sharing a moment that resolves us both. In that fundamental sense, the agency of each expands far more deeply into the other's movements as facilitator, enabler, and co-characterizer. That personal level of relational significance enables us to "get more out of life." The obverse is sometimes true too. A recent widow lamenting her loss might say that "she's lost part of herself." Agentively speaking, that is exactly what has happened to her.

We go on to explore how we can illumine the meaning of friendship in terms of shared intentions and enhanced agency. Our recognition of the primacy of the personal imperative leads us to expect that for a friendship to be viable, living in harmony with our friend's best interests must promise to actualize us most. Or, as we will abbreviate that mandate: We must be able to commit to our friend's best interests "in good faith." By tracing the conditions that the good-faith requirement puts on our relational life, I believe we can account for the intuitive feel we have for when friendships, including marriages, are healthful and when they are best broken.

In outline, the second chapter argues that

- Healthy interactions—those intended to add to the life of both parties—involve a shared intention.

- Shared intentions represent an expansion of the body of our intended movement and, accordingly, our growth as a person.

- The personal imperative—to actualize our intentional life as much as possible—draws us into interactivity by promising to actualize us more.

- When personal interactions succeed in actualizing two people's characters of resolve optimally, their friendship is personally compelling.

- But to be sustainable, it must continue to promise each partner's greatest actualization.

- Both the urgency of the imperative and the limitation it imposes determine the scope and meaning personal relationships can have for us.

Chapter 3 concerns the relative importance of what we do. Our argument to this point assumes that we can be aware of being personally incorporated, aware of moving with others as though in one body of movement. Moreover, it assumes that the way we are aware of incorporation makes it possible for us to assess its relative volume. To see how we are justified in making those assumptions, consider the formal truth about movements: They take time. We measure the movements made in acting by the time they take to achieve their intention. This temporal determination gives us our sense of an action's volume: It represents the combined moments of movement required for its achievement.

When we consider the various undertakings that we are resolved to achieve at any time, it is obvious that the body of movement achieving the character of our personal resolve cannot be explicitly qualified. That is because we cannot pay attention to it as a whole. We can only be aware of the greater body of our present action as the storied context for what we are attending to at the time. But we can imagine, at least vaguely, individual undertakings taking place in time, and we can at least vaguely imagine the course each might take to completion. Since the movement implicit in any resolute intention represents a multitude of such temporal spans, each according to the character of achievement intended, and since those spans can figure in our imagination—however vaguely and tentatively—it follows that our tacit awareness of the coordination for our life can be a sufficient basis for assessing the *relative* volumes of movement in the alternative courses open to us.

In ordinary language, we reflect this capacity for assessment when we judge some actions to be "of little moment" and others as "momentous." Our account is meant to provide a way to accredit philosophically what we affirm in ordinary ways of thinking: being who we intend to be obliges us to project the most momentous character of action we can.

This relative measure of moment is our basis for judging relative importance. In many contexts, we use "momentous" and "important" interchangeably, which testifies to the moment metric of assessment we find intuitive. It also discloses the logic of the word "important" as it refers to actions: What is being "imported" are the moments of movement we see implicit in how we characterize those intentions.

We will put this account of relative importance to the test by using it to describe how we deliberate about the course of action we should take in a given situation. We will see that judging relative importance in terms of relative moments of achievement nicely describes how we make decisions. Personal decisions about what is most important to do reflect our sense of what course promises to import the most meaning and moment into our life.

If the illustrations we will explore in chapter 3 bear out this meaning-movement-moment formula for personal importance, several doors open for us philosophically. One leads to a personalized understanding of practical reasoning. Typically, practical reasoning is represented as means-end reasoning: We have some end in mind, and we figure out the best means to achieve it. This is a time-honored account, but though it describes many of our moment-to-moment practical decisions, it does not describe how we deliberate when our decisions involve greater scopes of achievement. In those more important deliberations, our reasoning can be best defined as means-end*s* (plural) in form: We project a course (of resolve) that promises to best actualize our multiple intended ends.

To clarify means-ends deliberation, I am going to contrast it with the means-end reasoning Elizabeth Anscombe describes in her influential work *Intentions*. There she invites us to think of an act's intention as framed by the actor's answers to the question "Why?" A man is making up-and-down movements with his arm. Why? To operate a pump. Why? To replenish the household's water supply. Why? To poison the inhabitants. Why? To prevent bad people from seizing the reins of power. Why? To make it possible for good people to control the government and usher in the Kingdom of Heaven.[2] Roughly speaking, Anscombe's illustrations bear out the correlation we noticed earlier between the increasing importance of an intention and the increasing meaning/movement/moment it intends. The complications come with the recognition of the diverse intentions people often advance in doing what they do. When the pumper is represented as multi-intentioned, his action gains importance along registers other than the one indicated by his single linear succession of "Why?" answers.

By complicating Anscombe's account of intentions this way, we gain some traction for providing an account of personal deliberation. As its etymology indicates, "deliberations" draw inferences by "weighing." Let me suggest that what gets weighed are the relative moments of achievement that possible courses of action promise to advance. Our weighing can count as reasonable or unreasonable based on our imaginative ability to assess which option promises more actual moments of intentional satisfaction.

In outline, the third chapter argues that

- In intending to do something, we are aware of intending a body of movement that, in principle, has temporal measure. It is an achievement whose moment comprises the durations of the movements achieving it.

- Thus, courses of action are relatively momentous.

- Deliberations make relative judgments by imagining alternative courses of action to assess which promises to actualize us most. Those judgments can be seen to correlate with what we regard as the most important thing to do at the time.

- When we deliberate with multiple intentions in mind, our reasoning is means-ends in form.

- Such deliberation yields informed judgments about the relative volume of moment implicit in the alternatives before us. Thus, we can reasonably assess personal importance. Since it is implied in the character of action we assess, relative importance represents another dimension of an action's personal meaning.

Chapter 4 explores our awareness of relative moment to see how its permutations determine the ups and downs of our emotional life. To keep the moment/movement correlation before us, I frequently revert to its etymological root, *momentum*. Emotions register changes in *momentum*. Positive emotions like enthusiasm, joy, gratitude, and love are feelings of increased *momentum*, the inflation of agency; negative ones like fear, anxiety, and depression are feelings of decreased *momentum*, the deflation of agency.

To show how positive and negative emotions correlate with agentive activations and deactivations, we will look at how they connect on all three vectors of a person's agency—individual, interactive, and a third vector to be introduced, our actualization in the lives of those not interactively present. This third vector of meaning is what I call our action's "legacy" meaning. Because each vector represents movement determined in character by the character of our resolve, an increase or decrease in any of them can raise or lower our *momentum*. The positive emotion we will use to exemplify this dynamic is enthusiasm, particularly political enthusiasm. Our account leads us to expect that it will wax or wain according to how well candidates cultivate the agency of those they appeal to on all three agentive vectors. As we shall see, it does, and that gives us a useful way to think about political motivation.

Anger will exemplify negative emotion. Philosophers have long tended to think of emotion-driven behavior as irrational, and more than a few have singled out anger for special opprobrium. Stoics have urged people to dispel angry impulses by looking at what occasioned them from a rational perspective. In our own time, people continue to find that approach wise, since angry responses generally cause more harm than good. It is advice that endures and continues to be heeded.

But it is not wise advice in every situation. Sometimes it can be reasonable to react angrily. Our angry action qualifies as reasonable if two conditions are met. First, that the surge of anger we feel at some "slight" registers an actual loss of agency. If it does—that is, if we have not misinterpreted something as a slight that was not meant to be one—our anger counts as reasonable in the sense that it responds to an accurate discernment of interactive "belittling." Second, the angry action promises to actualize us most. There are circumstances, for example, when expressing anger is helpful in sustaining the health of a relationship. When both conditions are met—there is an actual slight and we can hope to prosper the relationship by acting angrily—then it is reasonable to act out of whatever intensity of anger is required to bring about that prospering.

Having recommended our change-in-*momentum* account as insightful in the way it leads us to describe emotional life, the chapter goes on to recommend it as useful in negotiating current philosophical discussions of emotions, particularly discussions about whether they are rooted in feelings or in judgments. Do our emotions cause us to judge as we do, or do our judgments cause us to feel the emotions we feel? The prevailing assumption is that we need a causal account of emotion one way or the other. That is an assumption I want to challenge by examining a type of causal argument exemplified recently by the work of a philosopher of cognitive science. By transposing its premises into the language and logic of agency, we preserve their collective force—which is to establish a cognitive basis for emotions—without resorting to a causal mechanism.

In outline, chapter 4 argues that

- Our *momentum* as agents rises and falls with the volume of movement we intend.

- Positive emotions register increased *momentum* and negative emotions decreased *momentum*.

- Understanding that dynamic allows us to describe specific positive and negative emotions insightfully.

- It also gives us a way to reconcile a current philosophical disagreement about the source of our emotions.

Chapter 5 considers how action takes on moral value. On the face of it, the topic seems to pose a problem for our account. Having established that every person is acting under an imperative to self-actualize as momentously as they can, it might seem that we have aligned ourselves with the position traditionally called "ethical egoism." True, we have seen that healthy interactions, particularly personal ones, can add greatly to the moment of what we do, and that they generally recommend themselves as personally advantageous for that reason. But there is a loophole: However richly our relational life contributes to the momentary meaning of what we do, it remains an open question as to whether healthy interactions are *always* personally advantageous. Our account as it stands leaves open the possibility that someone could attain the most meaning/*momentum* in life by exploiting others.

To see how we might reasonably plug that loophole, let us agree to assume that moral interactions are normally healthy. They are meant to benefit both parties. There may be special cases when using another person for some ulterior purpose is morally justified, but we can leave alleged counterexamples aside for now. It is enough for us to provisionally stipulate that healthy interactions have positive moral value and unhealthy ones negative moral value. To count as moral, an interaction must intend to be mutually edifying. If one party intends to exploit the other—to rob them of active possibility—then, in the absence of special considerations, the interaction is immoral.

Adopting this "healthy" requirement for moral interaction allows us to plug the loophole by defining the claim that, if we have grounds for believing it, exonerates us of the egoism charge. Consider: Our account leads to ethical egoism only if it allows for extending our agency by exploiting others. Clearly, if it were possible to intentionally exploit another and gain agentive advantage, our personal imperative would trump our moral imperative. We would likely have times when our moral imperative—to have only healthy interactions—would lose its unconditional status by virtue of losing its personal value. At such times, we could not in good faith recognize a personal obligation to be "moral." There is only one basis for denying that such times could arise, and that is to have reason for believing that *it is impossible ever to self-aggrandize at another's expense*. We must believe that only healthy relationships can reasonably be thought to edify us. That belief alone makes room for the authority of moral value as a personal value.

I am going to call this required belief—required to make morality a personal value—belief in "universal moral community," "universal" because it holds that no one can profit from exploiting another, "moral" because it qualifies under our healthy condition for moral interaction, and "community" because healthy interactions integrate the lives of the parties to them in ways that create community among them. Ultimately, whether moral value is always personally edifying depends on whether we have evidence for universal moral community (UMC).

Much of the discussion in chapter 5 concerns how someone might justify believing in UMC. If they come to find it reasonable, it must be because they can conceive of living in accord and in good faith with any person who did not intend them harm. In earlier chapters, by representing the role of intentions in coordinating movements, then representing the role of shared intentions in interactions, and then representing the role of sharing stories in a personal relationship, we discovered that each successive imaginative feat achieved in this developmental sequence was more comprehensive than its predecessor. That is because each adopted a more comprehensive level of accountability and intended a greater body of achievement. This pattern invites us to understand the question of whether it is reasonable to believe in UMC as a question about whether we can affirm UMC using the same standard of confirmation concerning the truth of any accountability commitment we make, namely by seeing whether we are aware of expanding our agency in taking on that expanded accountability.

We are going to see that at all levels of our interactive development, we follow the same pattern in confirming the reasonableness of our active relationships. A relationship is reasonable if the increased accountability that the interactors take on is more than compensated by the growth they enjoy in agency. As a belief, UMC obliges us to be accountable to a universal community of good-willed people—that is, of all people who intend only healthy interactions—so the confirmation of its reasonableness can only come with an awareness that living into that higher accountability enhances us personally. Whether or not it does can only be answered by us as an individual. If we commit to living in accord with UMC and find that membership edifying, we have evidence for regarding it as reasonable. In that case, we have a reasonable basis for assigning moral value: An action is moral if it promises to actualize the most personal *momentum* in the character of our resolve.

UMC is a belief with roots in many philosophical and religious systems. It continues to be embedded in our moral intuitions even if we no longer justify it with reference to those traditions. For that reason, it should be fruitful to examine how the dominant philosophical accounts of moral value appear in its light. Most ethicists take one of three positions on the matter: that an act's moral value is determined by its utility for creating happiness, that it is determined by its adherence to what reason determines as the actor's duty, or that it is determined by its accord with human virtues. What makes ethics classes so endlessly intriguing is that utilitarian accounts confirm our moral intuitions in some situations, but duty or virtue accounts do so in others. None of these three positions fully captures the logic of our reasoning in all moral matters.

I am convinced that we can break the impasse by transposing each account of moral value, restating the insights of each using the logic appropriate to reasoning about the character of action. By replacing the utility in occasioning happiness with the utility in creating moments of achievement, by replacing the categorical imperative with the personal imperative, and by thinking of virtues as habits of the optimally actualized, the insights of the three possibilities turn out to be mutually supportive. We derive a personalist version of utilitarian ethics, a personalist version of duty-based ethics, and a personalist version of virtue ethics, all congenial with one another.

Not only do the resulting compatible versions of utilitarian reasoning, duty reasoning, and virtue reasoning track better with how we make moral judgments, but they are also immune to the standard criticisms to which each has seemed vulnerable.

In outline, chapter 5 argues that

- Always acting in obedience to the personal imperative need not make us ethical egoists, not if we have reason to believe in universal moral community, which is to say in the assurance that every person, each in obedience to their own personal imperative, is able to resolve their actions with those of any interactor open to that healthy possibility.

- Belief in UMC has roots in a variety of religious and philosophical traditions and continues to inform the moral sensibilities of a great many people, even those who no longer justify it with reference to those traditions.

- While we cannot prove or disprove UMC with the impersonal reasoning of this account, we can describe the form evidence would have to take to confirm or disconfirm the belief on rational grounds.

- Those who do find the belief reasonable enough to live their lives trusting in its truth are able to adopt all three dominant ethical doctrines—utility-based, duty-based, and virtue-based—in a way that accommodates each's core insights without incurring the standard vulnerabilities critics charge them with.

Chapter 6 closes out this account of personal meaning by taking on that cliched yet profound question, "What is the meaning of life?"

We have seen that representing a person's projection of life's course going forward provides a portal into what their action means to them presently. It can also be used as a basis for addressing the question of life's meaning. That basis is to be found in the distinctive temporal logic appropriate to personal stories. The temporality of a personal story is distinctive in that it comprises past, present, and future actions. What we need to keep in mind is that the course traced from a past, through a present, into a future has its legitimacy because it projects our greatest success. Because we project resolve to optimize our *present* life, and our past and future life is determined by the way it serves that end, *who* we are is generated in the meaning of our active presence.

That casts a new light on the "meaning of life" question. The combination of conclusions—that we are only characterizable in our active presence and that our present character has a past and future—allows us to interpret the "meaning of life" as "momentary." By shifting the logic of "moment," we are not settling for the ephemeral identity that postmodern contingency accounts of meaning seem to glory in. They are predisposed by scientific-era thinking to hear "momentary" as "ephemeral," so the notion of life having only momentary meaning becomes paradoxical at best. To sidestep that path to depersonalization, we need to hear "momentary" in its active sense. Then no ring of irony sounds in the claim. Our active presence as a character of resolve understands our present moves as meaningful in a coordinated and coordinating context, narrative in form, spanning time, and identifying us as a protagonist. By transposing the "meaning of life" question into the appropriate temporal logic, we not only make it cogent, but we also ask it in a way that makes it answerable for every person.

Among the philosophical advantages to recognizing the meaning of life as a function of personal meaning is that we do not have to construe it as either subjective or objective. The meaning of an active moment detaches us from that dichotomy. Life's meaning is implicit in whatever character of action we are resolved on. Its richness is the product of the way it resolves those involvements and is resolved in them. If someone's life contained only their individual actions, its character would be so circumscribed as to be almost impersonal. If that person comes to be embodied with others in friendships, their life deepens in meaning. It deepens still further if the good acts they do promise to outlast them, reverberating to positive effect in others' lives. Finally, as we will have seen in the previous chapter, it is at least conceivable that one could live in the hope of acting in accord with all people of goodwill who are acting in good faith. This suggests a spectrum of possible personal answers to the question, one that reaches from a life of little meaning to one of ultimate meaning.

In outline, chapter 6 argues that:

- The question "What is the meaning of life?" makes sense if it is about personal meaning.

- Asking it that way makes life's meaning "momentary" in our expansive reading of that term, and it allows us to avoid calling it either subjective or objective.

- It also allows us to answer the question personally, based on the body of movement we act accountably to and share in the ongoing achievement of.

Allow me to make one more preliminary remark before we develop this account of personal meaning. By now, it must be abundantly clear that what I am proposing here represents a radical departure from the dominant professional ways people reason about people's actions. By highlighting the common ways that we characterize action without categorizing it, I am inviting the reader to resist some of the dominant habits of thought fostered in the modern scientific era. I am inviting you to do this partly by listening for pre-modern reverberations in the vocabulary we commonly use to discuss actions with personal meaning. These original meanings are what disclose the character logic we are using. They remind us of old but appropriately enduring habits of thought, ones that tend to get overshadowed in modern contexts but persist unashamedly in ordinary ways of reasoning.

In one respect, your deep familiarity with this reasoning should make it easy for you to follow what follows: You are already fluent in the character logic of the language it explores. In another respect, this account may puzzle you in spots. By reverting to these foundational meanings, I sometimes set up a cognitive tension with how we use those terms in most contemporary systematic contexts. We have already seen this with the words "moment" and "intention." I occasionally try to summon the resonance of the older usages by calling etymology into service. If this exercise in linguistic originalism becomes disorienting, you may find it helpful to consult the glossary at the end of the book.

1

Individual Meaning

I set out to isolate something distinctive about the personal meaning of an action, something deriving from the role multi-intentioned agency plays in determining its character. Because we can advance more than one part of our intentional life at a time, our action gets enriched in meaning by whatever multiple achievements it intends. As agents, we are most fully actualized when all we intend is moving toward completion as intended. That makes us motivated to coordinate our actions whenever we can. When we perceive our present action as counteracting other parts of our agenda, we suffer partial deactivation as an agent. This makes our relative personal success dependent largely on how well we continue to coordinate our intentional life.

We have observed how the process of coordination gets accomplished in occasional moments of resolve, moments largely built on the legacy of past moments narratively coherent with them. It is they that have served to accomplish us most in the past, and presumably it is they that will continue to characterize our life going forward. In this chapter we explore the sense in which that course, projected and retrojected, represents a "storyline." As does any storyteller, we project a course of action that puts actions together in new ways to meet new circumstances, overcome new obstacles, and seize new opportunities. Our life is punctuated by episodes of resolving ourself to meet new circumstances. If this describes how we meet the future, we should expect it to describe all our mindful decision-making, even decisions about mundane matters. We must expect to find an underlying aim to sustain overall coherence evident at every turn.

We find the logic of decision-making on display in the ordinary language we use when we reason about people and what they do. For instance, we say that actions have intentions and that persons do too. Notice how that word, "intention," draws actors and actions into a semantically symbiotic relationship. An actor's intentions are our only clues to *who* they are, and *who* the actor is is our only clue as to the personal meaning of their actions. Because "intention" is foundational in this account—humans being distinguished among agents as "multi-intentioned"—we had best pause to agree on how we use that word when we discuss personal meaning. First and foremost, we need to resist an old intellectual habit, one that can easily mislead us. "Intention" is one of those words that got appropriated and recommissioned in the modern era when intellectuals began thinking of it as something mental, like Brentano's "mental direction" or Frege's "propositional attitude." Modernity's propensity to treat minds in contradistinction to bodies led most intellectuals to file "intention" under "mind." What got lost in that translation was the *tension* part. To *in-tend* in the premodern sense is to *stretch-into*. Since "minds" as they are construed in modern philosophy take up no space, that etymological root had to be severed. No space, no "stretching." Because the mind/body dichotomy had come to inform the discussion and because the mind is a no-stretching zone, it behooved twentieth-century analysts to adopt as their paradigms of intentions ones achieved in a single move, indeed a move so short-spanned in its execution that it escapes notice as stretching over time and through space. They represented turning on a light as the intention of flipping the switch,[1] signaling a turn as the intention of raising one's arm,[2] or killing a man as the intention of shooting him.[3] What this approach did was to shift analytic discussions of intentions away from the long-stretching kind—like raising a child or learning to play the guitar—to virtually instantaneous ones. Since long-term intentions tend to be the ones that coordinate wider ranges of our intentional life, that approach militated against discussing the very intentions most transparent to the character identity of a person. The intentions we recognize as "resolute"—those that modify the character of our present intentional movement in the interest of more than one intention—got systematically overlooked, and with them the margin of richness we associate with personal meaning. In effect, they relinquished any personal context for characterizing people's actions.

To avoid that dead end, our discussion will stick to the common ways we refer to someone's intention, in terms of how we characterize their action, and of their action as being actualized in movement over time and through space. As we commonly speak and reason, when people behave intentionally, they are aware of what they are doing and characterize it in their awareness.

Since a description of a person's active awareness will serve as our portal into this account of personal meaning, we need to agree on some terminology for distinguishing facets of active awareness. We will describe the active awareness of a person as having three layers, the attentive, the adverbial, and the accordant, each of which we will examine in the chapter sections ahead.

1. The "attentive" meaning of what someone is presently doing is the meaning of the action they are paying attention to. It is typically characterizable with a simple category of action. For example, the attentive meaning of what the driver merging onto I-40 is doing can be characterized as "merging with the traffic."

2. The "adverbial" meaning is implicit in whatever modifications an actor makes to their attended-to action for the sake of coordinating it better with other elements in their life. The driver merging into I-40 traffic is gunning it to get to the beach sooner.

3. The "accordant" meaning of the adverbially modified attended-to action is the context of intentional accord an actor is trying to sustain in life. The driver is aware of speeding toward the beach with joy at the prospect of seeing her boyfriend.

To get at what is distinctive about each layer of personal meaning, it helps to observe how each functions in the process of integrating our life so that we can think of ourself as an individual.

How Action Comes to Have Adverbial Meaning

Jack and Jill are philosophy grad students with apartments on the same hall. One day Jill invites Jack for dinner. When he arrives and finds her absorbed in watching the news, he asks, "What are you doing?" Jill, sniffing in mock annoyance, says, "What does it look like I'm doing? I'm watching the news." Then, in a droll imitation of their philosophy of action professor, Jack strokes his chin pensively. "Yes, Jill, but watching the news surely doesn't exhaust your present agency. In the broader, present-continuing sense of 'present,' you must be presently doing a good many other things as well."

Jill, philosopher that she is, finds Jack's question intriguing enough to indulge in this bit of philosophical anthropology. In no time, she thinks of several things that she's doing in addition to watching the news. She's preheating the oven, nursing a sore back, hosting Jack for dinner, reading an Iris Murdoch novel, mulling a paper proposal due on Thursday, and ruminating on how she might teach her class on Sartre next week. Jotting them down as fast as she thinks them up, in no time she has a list of twenty.

Jill notices some common features among these twenty present intentions. Each is an item on her agenda at the present time, which is to say each is somewhere along its course from inception to completion as she projects it. Also, each item as she projects it represents movement though space and time; otherwise it would be (oxymoronically) an unintended action. Finally, she notes that at some level she must be aware of pursuing each; otherwise she couldn't have come up with the list.

Jill also observes some differences among her present intentions, differences in how she is aware of them. When Jack asks her if she was aware of preheating the oven just before he knocked at the door, she has to think through her answer. She hadn't been aware of it in the way that she was aware of watching the news. She was paying attention to the news but not paying attention to the timer. But neither was she oblivious to the fact that she was listening for the timer. She might have told Jack that "listening for the timer was in the back of my mind." "What about reading the Murdoch novel and planning the Sartre session? Were they in the back of your mind too?" "Yes," she replied, "but I guess I'd have to say that while I was watching the news, they were more remotely in the back of my mind."

The three-part distinction Jill is giving voice to here is what we are calling the attentive, adverbial, and accordant modes of her active awareness. First, there was what she was paying attention to doing. "What does it look like I'm doing? I'm watching the news." Usually bystanders can observe someone's action and name its attentive meaning. So Jack, if he'd been more perceptive, would have been able to characterize her action as "watching the news." Hence her sarcasm, "What does it look like I'm doing?"

As for her awareness of listening for the timer, awareness she describes as being in the back of her mind but not the remote back, it constitutes the "adverbial" meaning of what she was doing because it was implicit in *how* she was watching the news: Her aural guard was up, and she had lowered the volume to be sure to hear the buzzer. Nursing her sore back also made demands on how she watched: From time to time, it punctuated her attention by prompting her to shift her position to alleviate the ache, a shift that occasionally modified how she watched for a few seconds. Jill was aware of the adverbial meaning of watching the news by being aware of *how* she watched.

How Action Comes to Have Accordant meaning

Most of Jill's listed intentions are projects that she is neither attending to nor modifying her attended-to action in the interests of. These unattended-to parts of her agenda include her intention to finish reading the novel and her intention to prepare for leading the Sartre discussion. Their status in her awareness needs clarification if we are to maintain that whatever we intend, we are aware of intending it. Since listening for the timer and nursing a sore back affect how she is doing what she is paying attention to doing, but reading the novel and planning the session do not, Jill might accurately claim that she hadn't been thinking about the latter two at all. But thinking about and being aware of are not the same, which is part of what our threefold distinction is meant to highlight. If, in the middle of watching the news, someone asked her, "Are you still reading that Iris Murdoch novel?," she would not have hesitated to answer "yes."

How are we to understand Jill's present awareness of reading the novel? How can many of our agenda items be present in our awareness even when we are not thinking about them? What justification can Jill claim for saying that, even at that moment, she knew she was reading the novel and planning the discussion? An illustration can help us answer.

Fifteen minutes before Jack knocked on the door, Jill took advantage of a commercial break to look for some pain reliever. Reaching into the medicine cabinet, she found only an empty bottle. In frustration, she impulsively decided to head for the corner drugstore. But after a second or two, she caught herself. "Wait! Jack will be here any minute; I can't go now."

Consider those few seconds during which she began to move on her intention to go to the drugstore. If we asked her to describe her awareness during that brief time, she might report that she had momentarily forgotten she was hosting Jack, but then that commitment intruded into her attention: "Wait!" Consider what this intrusion into her attentive awareness implies about its presence during those few pre-intrusion seconds. The fact that it "got her attention" implies it was there to do the getting. Its intrusion proved that it had been continuing to exert operational authority over the way she conducted her life. In that sense, it must be that she had been aware of it all the time.

There is something else worth noting about this momentarily forgotten intention to host Jack. It was only one of the several "remote" elements of her intentional life at the time—she still intended to read the novel, for instance—yet it alone intruded into her attentive awareness. Why it and not one of the others? The answer is obvious, but telling for our purposes: Her intention to host Jack was the only one (out of the twenty) whose success was jeopardized by her short-lived intention to go to the drugstore. Put another way, by impulsively deciding to go to the drugstore, she initiated an action that would have counteracted her evening's activities as she had projected them. As soon as the jeopardized hosting intention reasserted itself, she knew it "wouldn't do" for her to be gone when he came.

Recall that the foundational premise of this account—deriving from our very nature as multi-intentioned agents—has to do with our impetus for continuing to resolve ourself anew. Jill's awakening—"Wait!"—can be read as evidence that she was being guided by her personal imperative to optimize the success of her agenda. If she had followed through with her intention to go shopping when Jack was due, she would have set her intentional life back by counteracting the course she had resolved upon. Yes, she would have satisfied her intention to relieve the ache, but only at the expense of something far more meaningful to her, the evening she had planned. Of course she still wanted to alleviate the pain, so it doesn't surprise us that she quickly followed up with another resolution, to enjoy a few extra glasses of wine that evening "for medicinal purposes."

Consider now that point in time when she realized that going to the drugstore would be personally defeating. How might she describe what happened in that moment? She might say something like "I just caught myself" or "I suddenly remembered." There is a reflexive grammar at play in statements like these. Such reflexivity is obvious with "caught myself," but it still echoes as well in an older usage of "remembered." Think of Lord Byron recalling, "I do remember me, that in my youth . . . I stood within the Coliseum wall." To "remember" refers to the same moment of sudden (personal) self-awareness that to "catch oneself" does. To remember is to restore to membership; her intention to host Jack was a member of the coordinated wholeness of Jill's life that evening, so it suddenly had to be remembered if she wasn't to suffer personal loss. Jill's quick renunciation of the drugstore intention illustrates how the prospect of a counteraction between what she was attending to and her overall normative coordination prompted her to modify her course lest she be damaged in her agency.

On other, happier occasions, intrusions come as positive prompts to take advantage of a situation. Recall that Jill, while she was watching the news, also had on her agenda teaching a class on Sartre. As she watched a pompous public figure being interviewed, his swagger struck her as the very epitome of someone in a state of awareness Sartre calls "bad faith." She was seized of that possibility and she seized on that possibility: "I can use this narcissist as an illustration in class!"

Both shifts in attention—that from heading out to the drugstore to stopping herself and that from watching the news to watching the news with an eye toward preparing a better class discussion—represent intrusive prompts to resolve Jill's agenda better by recharacterizing something she is doing. In the first case, two intentions threatened to counteract one another as presently projected, so she coordinated her intention to host Jack with her intention to relieve her pain by opting for a medicinal drink or two. In the news-watching instance, her resolve to use the interview in class modified both how she was watching and how she was planning to teach. Formally speaking, in each case she merged two projections of intentional movement into one course of coherent action, one that promised to advance her intentional life most expeditiously.

If we were to ask Jill to describe how she became aware of that pedagogical possibility, she might say something like "it just came to me" or "it just struck me." "It came to me" and "it struck me" both assume a source outside her attentional awareness from which it struck. They do not, however, assume that it came come from outside her agency, since it was *her* intention that intruded. The only way to account for it is to trace it to that sense of intentional accord she enjoys as the background for her attentional awareness. She does, that is, until the next intrusive warning of an impending contention to be avoided or alert to an advantage to be gained.

In an age of electronic metaphors, we are tempted to think of Jill's accordant self-monitoring as operating something like a keyword search: her cognitive computer subjecting each of the other nineteen intentions to test for counteractivity to the drugstore run, getting a hit on "having Jack over for dinner," then triggering the intrusion. But this processing metaphor is self-limiting. It ignores how the nineteen have been mutually modified in an extended series of accommodative moments of resolve. Instead of representing Jill's twenty present intentions as mutually coordinated, the computational model reckons with them as discrete meanings, each thus devoid of a personal context.

Our discussion up to this point has dealt mostly with quotidian moments of resolve, ones that involve relatively small subsets of our intentional life. But the imaginative capacity to resolve life is scalable. We sometimes have moments of reimagining great swaths of intentional movement in a novel way. Take Jill's resolution to undertake graduate school. That decision involved recharacterizing a great deal of her life, reimagining how she might achieve some of her ongoing intentions under new conditions. That is why we say that someone is "highly resolved" to do something when they have apparently modified a good deal of their life to accomplish it. The proof that Jill is highly resolved to get her PhD is that so much of her life is either being coordinated with it or sacrificed to it.

In summary, our account of being aware of what we are doing—what I am calling our active awareness—describes it as more than awareness of *an* intention. It is awareness of an intention normally nested in a coordinated agenda of multiple intentions. The moments of resolve in which this overall coordination is sustained include both big ones and little ones, rare ones involving great ranges of intentional life and more frequent ones of modest scope. This pulse of meaning-giving moments refining courses of action can be said to intend optimal personal achievement. Let us give a name to that confidence that we are leaning into our greatest actualization in how we are presently resolving our life. Let us call that confidence "good faith." For as long as we maintain good faith, the accordant meaning of our action provides a normative personal context for what we do.

In the Absence of Accordant Meaning

Because the source of the personal significance of what we do lies in the layer of accordant meaning, we cannot pay attention to it. We can, however, reflect on its presence in our awareness by considering some of the ways we become aware of its absence. We will look briefly at three types of occasions when we attend to doing something that has no personal meaning: times when we are absent-minded, times when we are weak-willed, and times when we dream of acting. These three examples of acting while deprived of accordant awareness might at least summon the ghost of its presence.

1) We commonly and appropriately use the term "absent-minded" to indicate both a loss of adverbial meaning and a loss of accordant meaning. The former loss is common, particularly in people of a certain age, but it can happen to the young as well. The other day, Jill walked into her bedroom to get her reading glasses but forgot what she was there for. Walking into the bedroom was intact as her intention—it coordinated her physical movement—but its meaning had lost its adverbial content. Hers was a normal fallibility, and though we like to tease people for such lapses, we don't often blame them.

The absent-mindedness we do blame people for occurs when no intrusion from their accordant awareness alerts them to a pending discord. For example, when Jill was supposed to begin teaching the Sartre session, she was sitting in her study cubicle, absorbed in a novel and oblivious to the time. Her absent-mindedness was the absence of awareness of how she was resolving her life, awareness she is obliged to maintain to sustain optimal resolve. That makes it *personally* blameworthy. Unlike the glasses-fetching failure—it bespeaks a personal failing in that what failed her was precisely what identified her, her character of ongoing accord. Her character of resolve failed to intrude on her reading. If she had been attuned to the personal meaning of her reading, she (again) would have "caught herself" and "remembered." What was blameworthily absent from her awareness was the sense of an integrated bearing to which she personally holds herself accountable. The price of vigilance is the cost of coherent life; we are thus obliged to pay it.

2) Another kind of action without accordant meaning is "akratic" action, as Aristotle called it, or "weak-willed" action, as we more commonly call it today. Weak-willed action draws more philosophical interest than absent-minded action, particularly among philosophers who hold a certain view about what motivates action. They say that we are motivated to act the way we do by an evaluative judgment we have made about that way of acting. The idea is that whenever I do something, I do it because I value doing it at the time. In effect, my evaluation constitutes

my imperative to act. As R. M. Hare saw it, "It is a tautology to say that we cannot sincerely assent to a . . . command addressed to ourselves, and *at the same time* not perform it, if now is the occasion for performing it and it is in our (physical and psychological) power to do so."[4] In effect, by having been enacted, an action testifies to having been valued above all others at the time. Critics have pointed out, however, that Hare's position has no basis for recognizing some actions as "weak-willed." Judgments cannot be what motivate actions because judgments are binary. There can be no weakness or strength to their meaning.

Dismissing the notion that some actions are "weak-willed" runs up against common sense. We intuitively blame some people who give in to temptation because we find it reasonable to think that, "deep down," they must have known it was wrongheaded to do so. If we could not assume "deep down" awareness, we could not justify blaming them for their negligence, recklessness, or thoughtlessness.

Jill offers Jack a second slice of blueberry pie à la mode. Jack is tempted, but he has put on thirty pounds since high school and has resolved to reign in the calories this year. That pie sure looks good though, and after a pause, he caves to the urge and reaches for the plate. "What the hell; you only live once." Later, though, he chides himself for his lack of willpower. Suppose Hare were there to console him: "Don't blame yourself, Jack. You were only doing what you thought best at the time." I doubt that Jack would feel absolved from his gluttony. He might even feel patronized. He knows that his flicker of remorse lights up his "better self" and thereby reasserts its governance over his agency.

Philosophers who hold the action-as-the-result-of-evaluative-judgment view might try to explain Jack's acratic action by pointing out that everyone has multiple motives, each based on a distinct evaluative judgment. Jack saying "yes" to the pie was due to his evaluation at dessert time; he felt remorseful about it later because another motive was making its judgment then. But this fallback position still does not justify blaming someone for their weakness of will.

It seems that we are left with no way to hold onto both items of common sense, that being weak of will is blameworthy and that evaluative judgments seem to guide our behavior. The *Stanford Encyclopedia of Philosophy* summarizes the current state of discussion: "What is required is a view which successfully navigates between the Scylla of an extreme internalism about evaluative judgment which would preclude the possibility of weakness of will, and the Charybdis of an extreme externalism which would deny any privileged role to evaluative judgment in practical reasoning or rational action."[5]

Let me suggest that we can navigate through that passage by using the resolute/irresolute distinction. Jack may be subject to many motivations, but only some of them are elements of his resolve. That distinction allows us to privilege the personal authority of resolved intentions and blame the others as weak-willed. Weak-willed action is action done apart from and contrary to the way we resolve our life at the time. It is weak in meaning and movement relative to the actor's personal life.

We are all weak-willed at times, and we seem to be so by nature. Unless someone is completely integrated as an agent, their intentional life comprises more actions than they find ways to include in the way they coordinate their life. That makes the temptation to act irresolutely inevitable. Paul of Tarsus had this in mind when he lamented, "Now if I do what I do not want" [read: "what I am not resolved to do"], "it is no longer I who do it, but it is sin living in me that does it" (Romans 7:20, *Common English Bible*). We can hear the apostle acknowledging that, strictly speaking, he is not *personally* responsible for his unresolved actions. We make that same point when we call weak-willed people and their behavior "irresponsible." The irresponsible actor's action is not the action of the person he is, since it lies outside the coherence he identifies with. He cannot be held *personally* responsible for his weak-willed action, but he is responsible for the weakness in his resolve that allowed for it. Instead of holding himself personally responsible for a harmful act, Paul holds himself personally responsible for the deficiency in his resolve, an offense against his personal imperative. That deficiency is his failing.

We make the same distinction in legal reasoning. If we hold a company's CFO responsible for embezzling funds, we imply that his embezzling was action in accord with how he was resolved at the time. That inclusion of the character of his action in the character of his personal resolve is what *implicates* him in his action: As a character of resolve, his identity is *implied* in the accordant meaning of his embezzling. On the other hand, when we accuse someone of acting irresponsibly, say in sideswiping another car while speeding on an ice-glazed highway, we do not see her personal responsibility extending to the sideswiping in the same way. Rather, we ascribe its occurrence to an unjustifiable gap in her self-governance, one that allowed her to irresponsibly drive without taking the icy road conditions into account. We refer to that gap with a verbal absence marker, calling her action "reckless" (without reckoning), "thoughtless" (without thinking), or "careless" (without caring). She is guilty because her action revealed an unnecessary weakness in her personal resolve.

3) Finally, let me suggest that it can be useful to think about dreaming as a way of characterizing action without giving it accordant meaning. When we are awake, we normally have no trouble distinguishing real-life action from dream-life action. Curiously though, accounting for that ability has proven challenging since the beginning of modern philosophy. Descartes doubted that any of us can ever be *certain* that we are not dreaming. (Of course, given his philosophical method of doubting everything dubitable, he had to say that.) Nonetheless, he was honest enough to admit to being confident that he was not dreaming, and in the *Sixth Meditation* he ventured to lay out the basis for his confidence:

"But when I perceive objects with regard to which I can distinctly determine both the place whence they come, and that in which they are, and the time at which they appear to me, and when, without interruption, I can connect the perception I have of them with the whole of the other parts of my life, I am perfectly sure that what I thus perceive occurs while I am awake and not during sleep."[6]

For Descartes, the mark of a real-life perception is the web of connections among the perceptions it is caught in. Descartes was a good phenomenologist on this matter, and we concurred with his description (in our own terms) when we noted how our acts are connected *in meaning* by their adverbial modifications and how we intend (without being able to attend to) our overall coordination whenever we mindfully resolve to do something. Alas for Descartes's point though. Once the discussion of perceptions got taken over by empiricists, it was conducted in the language of experience. Under that regime, the connectivity Descartes perceived had to be questioned. As Hobbes and Hume pointed out, nothing says one could not be mistaken about those experiential connections.

The way to vindicate Descartes's description is to transpose what he called connections among "perceptions" into connections among "characters of action." In our reading, awake-awareness is awareness of acting with accordant meaning, and that accordant layer is what distinguishes living contexts from dreamscapes. Dream actions may have adverbial meaning coordinating them within a dreamscape, but they lack accordant meaning. Happily, when we awaken, "it all comes back." We become *con-scious, with-knowledge*—which I am reading as *with-accordant awareness*—which is to say, with access to the tacit awareness of our agentive accord. The "it" in "it all comes back" is the "catcher" in "I caught myself."

It is us, our active context, the layer of accordant awareness that is now, once again, present as the tacit context for what we attend to.

The Storied Character of Personal Resolve

I have been describing the process of projecting personal identity as one of adjusting the courses of our action in a succession of occasional moments rethinking our way forward. We recalibrate the terms of our coordination so that we can continue to optimize our actualization. The adjustments we make—both in the many micro-decisions and in the occasional more movement-comprehensive ones—are meant to maximize the hold our resolve has over our intentional life.

Up to this point, I have said little about how it makes sense to talk about the coherence our acts of resolve aim to sustain, except to say that it is like, but in certain respects unlike, that of a conventional story. Since our account holds that the moments of our active awareness do not cohere as a succession of experiences, we need to say how they do cohere, and how we are aware of that coherence. So let us consider some features of the meaning coherence has for us when we are mindful, strong-willed, and wide awake.

We took the first step toward providing that description when we acknowledged that whatever form personal meaning takes, it can have no other source than those episodic moments in which we resolve our actions anew. Since each such moment projects an accommodation among a subset of our then-present intentions, and since we can usually depend on an intrusion into our attentive awareness by any threatened intention or any intention standing to gain from being projected anew, the picture that emerges is one of persons building and supporting overall harmony in their active lives. It is in the context characterizing that accord that *actions* have *personal meaning*.

If the context that gives our actions personal meaning is narrative in form, yet, as I cautioned, crucially unlike the narratives of conventional stories, we must specify how they are disanalogous. We can begin by noticing the distinctive temporal structure of any narrative that can claim to contextualize personal meaning. It must relate future actions as well as past ones. Conventional stories are told exclusively in the past tense. Cinderella went to the ball. She danced with the prince. She left behind her slipper as she fled at midnight. The prince tracked her down. The slipper fit. . . Even actions projected into the future are related in the past tense: "And they lived happily ever after." In contrast, a personal story projects the most promising way forward, the one that promises to be the best way to go about getting done all that we presently intend to do. It is the narrative projection of an active future.

Personal stories also relate past actions. They must, since most of our present agenda items have a history without which they have no present character. Our story must retroject a history inscribed by some of our earlier acts of resolve, specifically those that have narrative continuity with our present resolve. It is they that normally inform patterns of accommodation that promise to work best for us going forward.

Our awareness of being present as a person is self-awareness as a being with a history. Moreover, we frame our identity in terms of a narrative essential to our greatest success as a multi-intentioned being. This account of the function of a personal story enables us to avoid two criticisms often leveled at narrative accounts of identity.

The first argues that if a story identified us, we could only be true to ourself by living it out, moving inexorably toward its determined end. We would be like one of those fated characters of Greek tragedy. Notice the past-tense-only assumption about personal stories underlying this criticism. Given the past-present-future temporal structure of a personal story, this criticism does not apply. The past of our personal story does not resolve our future. Rather, we resolve our future using that part of our past that continues to promise success in supporting how we resolve our life going forward.

There are also critics who buy into the notion of narrative identity but insist that we must think of that story as open-ended. The problem is that being open-ended is the same as being unresolved. An unresolved story would not be a story. Rather, it would be a mere chronicle, a recital of successive occasions without any closure, like a ship's log or a rainfall chart. By definition, it could not function to resolve someone's life. Given that we project a coherent narrative going forward as our means of resolving life, identifying as a story without a resolution would be counterproductive as well as oxymoronic.

The way we define someone's personal past—the past actions of the story that identifies them—sets it apart from their somatically indexed past—the past actions ascribable to their body. The latter set of actions is far more extensive than the former. Clearly, what our account stipulates as our "personal story" is the essential core of what we, more colloquially, call our life story. If you were to meet me and ask me about my past, I would probably tell you that I was born in Milwaukee (not an act on my part). I might go on to tell you how I washed dishes and peeled potatoes in a German hotel one summer (not a past act particularly useful to me for figuring out how to proceed with my life now). The point, though, is that while these elements are of my somatically indexed past, they are not essential to how I project myself now.

Again, we necessarily have a past that is essential to our story because most of what we presently intend was begun in the past and modified over time to sustain its harmony with other intended achievements. Such patterns of mutual accommodation have been established in earlier moments of resolve, and some of them (ordinarily, most of them) persist as modalities of satisfaction honed over the years: how we balance our work life, our leisure time, our friendships, and all the other responsibilities and avocations we are engaged in. For as long as any habit of accommodation continues to actualize us most fully, it would be folly to discard it in some grandiose Sartrean gesture proclaiming freedom from the past, as though we could best execute each moment of resolve de novo. We see evidence of this in the testimony of amnesiacs who feel diminished and unstable in their identity without a past. They yearn to discover their past because it is instrumental in informing *who* they are now.

To recap: This account of personal meaning is implicit in the multi-intentioned nature of human agency. It depicts persons as self-actualizing projects, narrative in form, and imagined episodically from moment of resolve to moment of resolve. In those pulses of agentive vitality, we intend to advance our life coherently without ever being able to attend to our story as a whole. But the episodes we project sustain a sense of overall accord, or at least as harmonious a life as we can manage. We presume the presence of that accord because we know when we are discordant with it. When we act mindfully—monitoring our action for its fit with our overall coordination—our action takes on the contextual significance of that coherent course. We have likened it to narrative resolve and called the context that makes meaning personal a "personal story."

Various Ways We Pay Attention to What We and Others Are Doing

Before we go on to explore various facets of personal meaning—relational significance, relative importance, emotional force, and moral value—I want to sound out the plausibility of this account in another way, by looking at what it implies for our active attention as a person. It stands to reason that if a personal imperative is at work in prompting every iteration of our story, we should expect to find it directing and redirecting our active attention whenever what we attend to has personal meaning.

To keep things in perspective, it helps to exclude certain kinds of attentive awareness from our interest here, namely any attention to actions that have no personal meaning. That would include reactions to things we are surprised by, like a butterfly alighting on a garden flower or the screeching of a weather alert on our device. It would also include elements of our active agenda that are executed out of accord with our personal resolve. There has been a growing appreciation, largely stemming from the psychoanalytic traditions, of what Jung called our "shadow self." In our terms, our "shadow self" motivates things "we" do, but the "we" refers to action somatically indexed, that is, inclusive of all the actions attributable to the body we are. So, yes, my shadow self is determining elements of my intentional life, but since these elements do not bear accordant meaning, they do not bear personal meaning. In that respect they are like the absent-minded, weak-willed, and dreamlike acts we discussed earlier.

What we are concerned with are the occasions when we mindfully turn our attention to something we or others *are doing*, be it frying an egg, maneuvering into a parking space, planning a shopping trip, reminiscing about a junior year abroad, or speculating about how artificial intelligence might change life on earth. Sometimes the attended-to action is a task at hand, other times it is something we did in the past, or had plans to achieve, or fancied doing in the future. In listening to Mozart, we pay attention to what he *did* in that passage. In watching a movie, we attend to how the actors are *acting*. In talking with someone, we take in what their speech acts are *telling us*. The span of our attention to such actions varies greatly too. Sometimes we do a succession of things that demand only short bursts of attention. Other times, we sustain our focus for a long time on an exacting task. Sometimes we "multitask" and our attention toggles among projects. Sometimes our attention seems to drift, for instance when we daydream.

Can there really be a logic controlling all this variation? Most people, I suspect, doubt that there is any rhyme or reason to the ways we shift our attention. They might attribute them to the ebb and flow of sundry demands from the cacophony of wants and needs conditioning our active existence. But given what we have seen of the nature of human agency, we are led to expect reason if not rhyme figures in how we come to direct our active attention as we do. The hypothesis we must test is this: *We pay attention to whatever part of our agenda needs our attention if we are to actualize ourself most fully in the moment, and we hold our attention that way for as long as that status holds.* One way we can confirm or disconfirm this hypothesis is to consider our sense of accountability for the times we fail to exercise that executive function. Our question is, do we find that in acting mindfully—with awareness of all three dimensions of the action's meaning—we direct attention from act to act to maximize the movement we are determining in character by our resolve, and do we blame ourself when we do not? To reason our way to a conclusion, we will consider several agentive conditions under which we direct our attention:

a) All of us who lead at least moderately complex intentional lives occasionally feel compelled to attend to some conflict that we sense is impending among our agenda items as we presently project them. We will call these conflicts "contentions" to emphasize what the etymology suggests, that two of our intentions, if enacted as intended, will run *contrary* to one another so that they determine our future course in counteractive ways. Think of how Jill's intention to host Jack contended against her intention to go to the drugstore: The latter would have determined the character of her movement in a way that precluded advancing the former successfully.

When we find ourself in such a situation—with two presumptively prevailing intentions putting us on a collision course—the imperative requires us to pay attention to that conflict lest we be defeated in our ambitions. Provided we have our wits about us, that is what we do. We pay attention by trying to imagine the best resolution to the situation. We have several strategies at our disposal. Sometimes it works best to defer one contender in the interest of the other, other times to modify one to accommodate the other, and still other times to modify both. Our aim in every case is to achieve the greatest overall success. The act called for is a projection of fresh resolve, since if we do not refresh the character of our action we will suffer deactivation.

Jill is leading the Sartre discussion. It's going well; everyone is absorbed, including Jill. In fact, she's so absorbed that when she glances at the time, she's brought up short. Ten minutes left and she still hasn't gotten to her newscast-inspired illustration. She intends to end the session on time—she has no choice; another class has the room booked—but she's also intent on showcasing her pedagogical pièce de résistance. Quickly moving to cut short the thread of discussion, she works in a short version of the illustration before wrapping it up. In other words, "on the spur of the moment" she modifies how she conducts the class (redirecting it and speeding it up) and how she presents her example (by doing it in abbreviated form), thus accommodating the two contending courses as well as she can. Had she not stopped in her teaching tracks to modify the last ten minutes of class, she would have left *disappointed, dis-appointed* from an achievement she had *appointed* for that hour, namely to illustrate Sartre's idea in the way she had prepared. If she had never gotten to that bit, she would have been momentarily diminished as a teacher, and she would have felt disappointment in that loss of agency.

Happily, the type of situation Jill faced in the example above is unusual for her and for most of us, I suspect. We would feel bad for anyone who dealt with it continually, either because of what they did for a living—like managing a political campaign or serving as a nurse during a pandemic—or because they lived in poverty, displacement, or otherwise fragile living conditions. Some people are seldom free from immediate problem-resolving, but to live that way—with hyper-attentiveness to the immediate—is agentively debilitating. That is because the long-term projects that give our story its narrative arc also need attention if they are to continue to cohere.

b) Imagine that right now we are unaware of any items on our agenda needing attention; we sense no immediately impending counteractions among the elements of our intentional life. We do however foresee the possibility of an eventual conflict in the days or weeks ahead. One of our aimed-for achievements, x, looks as though it might get in the way of another, y, given the way we presently project achieving each. The threat of counteractivity also constitutes a threat to our agency in that it projects an incoherent future, one that cannot claim to optimize us. While we are only aware of it as a possible future conflict, it would "undo" us if came to pass. For that reason, our anxiety—our awareness of the threat of being diminished as an agent—compels us to attend to imagining ways to head it off.

This mode of paying attention to our life—paying attention to perceived future contentions—is inevitable given the way new contingencies continually reshape our active possibilities. Our best-laid plans may need rethinking if we are to project them realistically under the new conditions we imagine on the horizon. Paying attention to such matters, what we commonly call worrying, is altogether appropriate as a strategy if it holds promise for achieving our greatest overall personal success. Our imperative requires that sort of vigilance, since occasional anticipatory course corrections may be needed to prevent snarls. Here, too, we blame ourself for problems that arise if we fail to attend to matters proactively, a sign of our recognition that we have disobeyed the imperative. Jill, for instance, kicked herself for not having thought ahead, watched the time, and paced the class discussion to better effect.

Recognizing that it is the imperative prompting us to worry also defines worry as inappropriate if it holds no prospect of heightening agentive success. When the conditions for our life going forward are taking shape beyond our control or even foreknowledge, it is a "waste of time" to concern ourself with them. When such unproductive worrying becomes habitual, it can become debilitating. Listen to how Reinhold Niebuhr's serenity prayer eloquently parses the possible arenas of our active life: "God grant me the serenity to accept the things I cannot change, the courage to change the things I can, and the wisdom to know the difference." The imperative is what draws that line.

c) Another kind of attention is called for when we confront an exacting task. We call it "undivided" attention or "concentration." To *concentrate* is to bring awareness of an action to a single center. It is, in our terms, to advance a project with no adverbial or accordant significance. In an archer's Zen moment or in the fraught awareness of an attorney fielding questions before the Supreme Court, the concentrated attention called for is one that exhausts the actor's active awareness.

Imagine an Olympic athlete poised at the start of her event. She may be living in her greatest personal moment. As we watch her perform, we not only thrill to her physical grace, we also admire her intense concentration. In the moment of her greatest personal achievement, she can "shut it all out." One way to describe her feat is to say that she momentarily disengages the personal meaning of her action, depersonalizing the character of her movement for the sake of an achievement she has been personally resolved upon for years.

We have been looking at three sets of conditions under which we pay attention to what we are doing—resolving an immediate conflict, heading off a future one, and concentrating on some particular action requiring "undivided" attention. Each of them projects a course that promises our greatest agentive success. All of them are "creative" in the sense that, by so directing our attention, we create the most present movement along the course we are resolved upon.

It has probably occurred to you that these uses of active attention, the "creative" ones, only account for a fraction of our active attention. If we are lucky enough to enjoy relatively stable lives, much of our active awareness is, rather than creative, "recreational." We are germinating meaning, but in a deferred way. I can think of two conditions—both must be met—that would justify us in projecting action recreationally. It is worth considering them because they draw the line we recognize separating a legitimate use of time and a decadent use.

The first is that nothing on our agenda needs attention because nothing needs modifying. We are not beset by impending crises, troubled by possible future ones, or involved in anything needing concentration. As far as we can tell, the coast is clear to continue advancing our agenda as presently projected. Second, it must be plausible to think we can foster a more creative active life by dwelling in them. Doing so must promise to nourish our imagination and thus feed our capacity to resolve future actions more effectively. Whenever both conditions are met, we are justified by the terms of the imperative to cut our attention loose from our agenda and take flights of fancy. We are free to entertain projections of movement determined in character by something other than our own projects.

d) One such recreational activity is dreaming. Dreamers—daydreamers and sleep dreamers alike—imagine acting in ways disengaged from accordant meaning, but a different kind of disengagement from that which we achieve in concentrating. In dreams—both asleep dreams and daydreams—we let accordant awareness slip away without intending to. In fact, trying to fall asleep usually keeps us awake. In dreaming, we typically have agency. But we act impersonally, which is why we take no personal responsibility for what we dream of doing. Without accordant meaning it was not *our* action in the personal sense, not the action of the person we are.

What about the second condition? Can we ever be said to have a personal imperative to dream? Can personal welfare mandate dreaming? Apparently so. People denied REM or dream sleep become anxious and depressed.[7] Analogous to how our body needs sleep—a period of intention-free movement—our agency apparently needs periods of resolve-free movement. Freud, Jung, and others have tried to diagram the plumbing of that utility, but our purposes do not require any blueprint. It is enough to know that people suffer personally when they are prevented from dreaming. For whatever reason, the road to greatest actualization traverses dreamscapes. Since we function optimally when we dream lavishly, dreaming can be justified as an imperative-driven use of our time.

e) I suspect that for most people, most recreational activity comes in attending to what others do or have done. We dwell in others' actions vicariously when we kibbitz at a chess game, follow a discussion, watch a movie, or read a biography. In each activity we attend to others' projects. If the imperative is said to be motivating us here too, it must be reasonable to believe that we can find agentive value in such characterization.

One thing seems evident. It was true of us while we were growing up. We developed as agents largely by imitating others. In following their projects, we enlarged the repertoire of active life patterns that we could then use to project our own actions more creatively.

But can the same be said for us as mature persons? It is fair to ask for evidence that our recreational activities can edify us agentively, albeit in a deferred way. And this leads us to ask how we register edification in our active life. How do we know when yielding creative control over our attentiveness stands to enrich our life? Let me give two answers to that question. One is a formal, trivial answer; the other a practical, instructive one. It trivially follows from the connection we discovered earlier between the amount of an intended action's movement and the richness of its meaning. As a formal matter, provided Jill's "twenty" present intentions all feel coordinated and none of them need her attention, adopting a twenty-first intention—watching *Jeopardy*, say—would add to her life in the moment in a minor way: For thirty minutes her watching would add to the body of movement she is presently intending.

The more interesting, practical answer is that recreational imagining at its best provides a vehicle for recognizing the form of personal coordination we aspire to. I am particularly thinking of storytelling that resolves a complex of episodes over a stretch of time. The story resolves a manifold of movements as perfectly as possible. Paradigmatically, literary works of art attempt to make coherent sense of the myriad episodes, character developments, and relationships they relate.

The first stories many of us heard as children were often stories of a single achievement, like *The Little Engine That Could*. We grew in our capacity to imagine coordinated actions by following the more complex stories we heard, and we observed which projects worked to the advantage of the characters and which did not. Eventually, when we heard tales purporting to grasp their protagonist as a whole person, we came to see its narrative form as akin to the form our resolve takes. By spinning threads of achievement that draw themselves into narrative coherence, a work of literary art can evoke the accord we seek to claim as the character of our individuality.

Given the formal affinity narrative resolve has with personal resolve, literature suggests itself as a prompt for every adolescent's personal project. But it is not just stories that function this way. A great many of what we call the "fine arts" aspire to complete an integration of the movements they comprise. We see and hear the integrity of their movement complicated in ways analogous to how our lives are complicated. The artistic project unfolding advances like ours, seeking coordination by resolving as it goes. Like persons, works of fine art come together by weaving what they spin. We call them "works" because they accomplish something singular—a display of their elements as parts of a whole—much as our intentional movement is projected as a meaningful whole. We find the arts "uplifting" because they lift us into the formal possibility of our own integrity.

To summarize: Projecting personal meaning for what we do is mandated by our nature as a multi-intentioned agent. In any active moment, we attend to some achievement. When it is our own, we often mindfully modify our execution of it to fit with the rest of our agenda. These little acts of resolve progressively constitute and sustain global coherence in our agency. In every instance of characterizing what we do resolutely, we advance that overall character of resolve episodically, intending an accord to which we are both committed and accountable. The character of that accord contextualizes what we do in a type of narrative that gives our action personal meaning.

So much for the basic character-of-resolve account of what gives actions personal meaning. I trust that the elements of it will become clearer as we explore the several features of it cited in the book's subtitle, the first of which is the relational significance our action can have.

Relational Significance

We turn now to look at how our actions come to have relational significance and at why we find so much depth and richness in them. We can answer those questions based on what we discovered in the previous chapter. There we found our tendency to strive toward assuming character identity implicit in the kind of agent we are: We must coordinate as much of our intentional life as we can to actualize ourselves most fully. This feat requires us to be aware of the volume in the body of movement we project and of the correlation between that volumetric body and the meaningfulness of what we do.

For our purposes, this way of identifying persons—as narrative achievements made actual in ongoing bodies of resolved intentional movement—stands in contrast to those of philosophers who follow John Locke. Because they identify a person as a set of *experiences*, their identity theories systematically ignore relational meaning. The task of defining personhood in terms of experience dictates that they specify the class of experiences attributable to a given person. Then the fun begins, for not only is there no obvious way to define this set of experiences, but the options all seem to entail paradoxes. That has left many agreeing with A. J. Ayer that we are left with the "unsolved logical difficulty of defining personal identity in anything other than physical terms."[1]

Our alternative approach to personal identity transposes claims about "the experience of acting" into claims about "the awareness of acting." That may seem a minor vocabulary adjustment, since "my experience of building a snowman" and "my awareness of building a snowman" may sound roughly equivalent. But there is a danger of sliding off into the wrong temporal logic unless we keep the difference in mind. Experiences happen at points in time while actions happen in durations of movement over time. Keeping in mind that difference in temporal logic will keep us on track for understanding the logic of our inferences about personal meaning.

We are of course masters in thinking both ways, aware of having experiences at points in time and aware of acting to achieve what we intend over time. The presence of other people in this dualistic temporal world depends on whether we are interacting with them. Persons with whom we are not interacting can be present *to* us as objects in our world, but when we interact with them, they are *with* us in the sense of "sharing the moment." Recognizing that awareness of interacting is awareness of sharing an active moment becomes awkward to acknowledge if we are committed to the experience model of identity. While two people can have experiences of the same type—they can both feel cold; they can both see something red—reasoning about experiences does not allow for saying that they are both having the *same* experience. My experience goes on in my head and yours in yours.

The kind of interaction that has positive relational significance is the kind I am calling "healthy," which is to say intended by both parties to benefit both parties. In that sense, healthy interactions involve "shared intentions," given that both parties intend their mutual benefit. Since this is such a foundational term in our account, we need to look closely at what we assume when we call behavior "intentional." The term is foundational because it is our movements' intention that makes it action. Action involves movement, but movement does not necessarily constitute action. To be action, movements must be coordinated to achieve some intention. To perceive someone acting is to perceive them coordinating moves to achieve something we can characterize. Our characterization of that achievement identifies both the act and actor's intention. Looked at from the inside, we can say that an intention is present in our awareness as the *ordination* of a *co-ordination* we achieve. We find no meaning in anyone's movement unless we recognize it as coordinated around some characterizable achievement; we discern no coordination apart from grasping the intended character we see the action bearing.

Invigorated by this round of linguistic gymnastics, let us look back to our notion of a healthy interaction to see how it involves a shared intention. When we see two people interact in a healthy way, we assume that they are not only advancing their individual agendas but that they are coordinating the achievement of them with one another. That coordination is their shared intent, an intent to advance both parties' individual aims. To keep things tidy definitionally, let us recognize all "interaction" as healthy. When two people act and react toward one another in ways that intend only their individual intentions, we will discount their exchange as a "transaction." My sense is that drawing the distinction this way reflects our common understanding of transactional relationships.

In the pages ahead, this analysis of interaction—as movement coordinated by a shared intention—is going to prove descriptively insightful and philosophically helpful, largely because of what it implies about the agentive growth it involves. Starting with the idea that the body of our personal action includes all the movements determined in character by our resolve, it becomes reasonable to count our shared intention (whose character we co-determine) as an extension of our agency. Both parties, by how they intend to interact, can be said to coordinate a body of achievement comprising more than their individual movements. In effect, each appropriates that greater body of movement as part of their agenda. In their moments of interacting, they are momentarily greater in the scope of their respective agencies.

The implication that our personal agency is expandable and contractible challenges a deeply ingrained habit of modern systematic thought. For several centuries we have been taught to regard every person's agency as limited to the actions of their physical body. In contrast, by construing a person's agency as the resolution of their intentions, we include as part of their agency intentions they share with others. If that sounds exotic, consider it from a wider historical perspective. Our modern habit of thinking of a person's actions as limited to one body's movement represents a relatively recent detour in intellectual history. Ancient people and pre-literate people often documented a strong sense of corporate identity. For example, the ancient Israelites personified their tribes—Benjamin, Judah, Dan—and rendered proper names in lineage contexts with all those "begats." Their tribal and familial histories identified them, and all other ancient peoples, in terms of corporate membership. It also obliged them to organize their lives, far more than we do, around advancing their common life.[2]

Ancient corporate personal identity was given a different twist in the Christian era when the Church proclaimed itself the Body of Christ and individuals saw themselves as members of it. A few centuries further along, this doctrinal version of corporate awareness was adopted and adapted as an instrument of political solidarity. In Christendom, the whole nation accepted the king as bearing their corporate identity. In effect, he had two bodies, his natural one and one that embodied the nation, a body-politic personified. It was bad theology but good politics. In more recent times, corporate identity has proven an even more suspect conceit, as fascists feed on our ontological penchant for wanting to be embodied in a character of resolve greater than our own.

The realization of how demonically corporate identity can wield power should not, however, prevent us from recognizing its legitimacy as a vector of our agentive being. Otherwise, the prevailing insular-with-set-boundaries model will lead us to ignore what I take to be our intuition in the matter. Specifically, a transactional model of interaction militates against recognizing the three-way correlation we discovered in the last chapter: The richer the meaning of an action, the greater the volume of movement intended, and the greater our sense of personal achievement. Because the three features rise and fall together in interactive solidarity, we are aware of moving in a greater body of action, one that expands the scope of movement determined in character by our resolve.

Our objective in the sections ahead is to understand what goes on in their active awareness when people interact—when they close a business deal, play bridge, engineer a corporate takeover, or just enjoy each other's company. My objective is to determine whether we can reasonably describe them as registering a joint body of interactive movement, one that enriches their active life and enhances their sense of agency.

Before we start, there is one more generic feature of our awareness of interacting we need to take into account: Interaction enjoins upon us widened accountability. Moving in accord with our interactor makes us accountable for facilitating their success as well as ours, since our success depends on them as well as us. To the extent that we are (momentarily) incorporated in the greater body of our coordinated movement, we are presumably accountable to seeing it through to completion.

Together, this set of correlations spells out the rudimentary character logic of relational meaning: its richness of meaning—"Being with her 'means' a lot to me"—is correlated with its enhancement of our agency—"She is part of my life"—is correlated with its entailment of increased accountability—"I feel responsible for not letting her down." The next step is to test whether the correlation makes descriptive sense when we apply it to concrete cases. Since the formula pertains to both impersonal and personal interactions, we will look at the reasoning leading to confirmation on the impersonal level first. Active meaning is less complicated there. Starting with a few ordinary, everyday examples of interacting impersonally, we will see whether the extended body of shared intentional movement correlates with how much the interaction means to us, how accountable we are to our partners for carrying it through, and how accomplished we feel in achieving it.

Impersonal Interaction

When we relate impersonally, we coordinate our actions around a specific course to which we and our interactor are jointly given, and we recognize mutual accountability only to completing that jointly intended course. Our limited commitment—limited to the shared achievement—makes the intention we share impersonal. Its character for us is not informed by the other's personal resolve.

Jill stops at the drugstore to pick up a bottle of pain reliever, finds it on the shelf, and brings it to the counter. The clerk scans it, bags it, and processes the receipt. Jill's intention to purchase the product could not be achieved without the cooperation of—the coordination of movement with—the clerk. His intention to carry out his job-related duty could not be achieved without Jill's cooperation in scanning her credit card and picking up the package. But that was the end of it. The accountability of each to the other was limited to carrying the purchase through; neither party had any intent to advance other parts of the other's life.

Impersonal interactions are not always isolated events with strangers, like Jill's with the clerk, so we should look at a few examples of more extended ones as well.

Jack and Jill, the philosophy grad students living across the hall from one another, are getting better acquainted. A year has passed and one of them broaches the possibility of sharing an apartment. When a two-bedroom unit becomes available near campus, they talk it over and agree to set up joint householding. They agree to share certain responsibilities in arrangements that seem advantageous to each. By agreeing to split the dog walking (they had both previously walked their respective dogs every morning), to share internet and streaming service fees, to take turns doing the cooking and dishes (each had done both daily), and to alternate in doing the weekly housecleaning, they each stand to save time and energy. It probably overstates things to say that their collaboration would cut the efforts of each in half (cooking or cleaning for two is marginally more arduous than for one, and walking two dogs is a little more taxing than walking one), but Jill is confident that she'll get done more of what she wants to do under this arrangement. Things she had wanted to do but could not intend to do (since she didn't have the time) she can now put on her agenda. Instead of spending twenty minutes dog walking every day, she can devote that time on off-days to reading Murdoch. That makes it reasonable for her to think that her life will be enhanced by this arrangement even though the world of her accountability extends to include the care of Jack's dog. It also seems reasonable to say that Jill will continue to regard the arrangement as a good one for as long as her increased accountability to Jack and his dog continues to sustain an increase in what she can expect to achieve.

So far we have assumed that, though Jack and Jill have become increasingly acquainted, their relationship remains impersonal. Their accountability extends only to a few discrete elements in their respective intentional lives, the ones that they have negotiated. Though they live in the same apartment, they lead largely separate lives. One cooks for both but they eat alone, she at her desk, delighting in the clarity of G. E. M. Anscombe; he at his, underlining his dog-eared Levinas. Aristotle would describe theirs as a friendship of convenience; each uses the other's active movements to further actualize their own intentional life, and each has accepted its cost in expanded accountability.

Personal Interaction

Months have passed, and Jack and Jill's relationship has "grown." (Notice how appropriate that volumetric word sounds here.) Over time, they have come to discern wider areas of one another's life, so that now something of the contextualizing coherence of the other's life is emerging. Each is becoming a character of resolve to the other much as a character in a novel does, little by little, accommodation by accommodation. Finally, glimpses of an overall individuality of character is intimated in every episode. Some specifics of their respective lives remain hidden, to be sure, but because each assumes that the other, like them, is aiming at coherence, they both assume that what they see emerging is really *who* the other is.

At this point, we can say that Jack and Jill have become "personally acquainted"; they are aware of personal meaning in what the other does. Shall we call them personal friends? To be sure, we tend to use word "friend" broadly. For instance, I have Facebook "friends" whom I haven't seen in decades and barely remember. For the purposes of this account, however, I am going to reserve the term for those who hold themselves accountable to one another's personal well-being. That is the level of accountability, I would suggest, we expect from "true" friends. What distinguishes them from even close personal acquaintances is our expectation that they are committed to always interact in accord with our interests as well as theirs. Personal acquaintance can be best thought of as a condition for friendship, but beyond having a good working knowledge of the other's agenda, both must agree to interact only in accord with how the other's agenda is being resolved. They must agree never to relate in ways that defeat the other's optimal actualization if, in good faith, they can help from doing so.

This commitment allows for friendships ranging from intimate to casual. With some friends, we interact often and derive greater meaning for our life in their presence. Other friends we see so rarely that we eventually lose the acquaintance that makes an active friendship possible. But what no friendship can ever lose is a mutual confidence in interacting that each intends to accord with the other's personal resolve, in effect to advance both their stories. That implied mutual understanding prompts a sense of betrayal we feel when a friend avoidably acts against our interests.

When we distinguish friends from acquaintances by that assumption of mutual commitment, it becomes apparent why we probably cannot be friends with all our personal acquaintances. Not everyone's personal story can be fully resolved with ours and ours with it. I do not mean to depict the decision to befriend someone as calculative, not explicitly anyway, any more than our other decisions about the best course going forward. The tacit nature of accordant meaning makes explication cognitively impossible, so we have to evaluate the other's promise as a friend in the same probative and probationary ways we feel for promising directions in our individual life. Our imagination must intimate possibilities before it can test them, and even then, confirm them only tentatively. Ontologically put, we befriend someone only when we see the promise of mutual agentive growth, a promise that can only be confirmed when our accountability to one another's personal resolve, and thus to their growth, yields expanded agency for us and makes both our lives more meaningful.

It is crucial that we keep that good-faith proviso in mind: I will act in accord with your life's projects *when I can do so in good faith*. That entailment of our personal imperative also determines when friendships need to be dissolved. Because the relationship makes personal sense only when it sustains the most promising life for them both, both must, on pain of sliding into bad faith, reserve the right to absolve from their relationship if it no longer maximizes their life in scope and significance.

In summary, our account of relational significance implies three general truths about friendship.

1. We are drawn into them by their promise to enhance both of our agencies.

2. Doing so requires, in addition to mutual personal acquaintance, a mutual commitment to interact in accord with the requirements of the other's greatest agentive success.

3. Friendships are sustainable for as long as, but only for as long as, both parties find them edifying in that way.

We have been looking at some implications that follow from recognizing our nature as multi-intentioned agents, implications for our relationships, particularly our friendships. Now that the formal definitions and distinctions are set out, it's time to test their descriptive power. Do these formal conditions square with the sense of accountability we operate with in our relational lives?

Consider first the experience of becoming friends. As we depicted it, the process involves moving from impersonal to personal accountability. Acquaintances are, of course, obliged to respect one another in the weak sense of not knowingly exploiting them. We can think of this as our social imperative, one based on what I take to be a consensus around the notion that a good society is one of healthy interactions. Our obligation to a friend runs deeper than that to a fellow citizen. Because we know something of the character of our friend's resolve, pursuing a healthy accord with them means acting to accord not simply with whatever shared intention is at hand but with what we know of how they project their life.

I mentioned earlier that the line between personal acquaintance and friendship should not be thought to preclude degrees of friendship. We can now see how a variable degree of interactive involvement accounts for that range. Friends sometimes lose touch, lose interest, or have a falling-out, or they just grow apart as they adapt to contingencies of fortune. It is an inevitable churn. "Losing touch" means attenuating the sense we have of the other as a character of resolve. There are fewer elements of that resolve, so the picture pixelates. The present other is unavailable. Only a past pregnant with the present other is preserved in memory.

If becoming friends means sharing a new level of accountability, that status needs to be mutually recognized and acknowledged. The ways this happens have ranged widely, culturally, linguistically, and generationally. Think of the romantic friendships in Jane Austen's country home world: Mutual understandings were negotiated with calling cards, furtive glances, and family conferences. In a 1950s high school, a letter sweater or an effusion of valentines might send a comparable signal. In current teen texting worlds, who knows? Every time and place has its own argot for marking the passage into that way of relating. Not that a relationship always gets affirmed with an overt gesture. Sometimes we simply rely on each other's friendship for long enough to presume to rely on it and to be relied on. Reciprocation makes the point in silence.

The process of getting to the point of mutually acknowledging personal accountability teems with comedic possibility. It can be fraught with strategic ambiguities, unpredictable fluidities, and stakes high enough to demand tentative moves. (When the stakes are the highest, we call the probationary period an "engagement.") Curiously, we English speakers have allowed ourselves to be disadvantaged in negotiating personal relationships. Along the way, we lost the use of the disambiguating pronouns that most languages provide. By using different pronouns for acquaintances than for friends, a speaker can signal an offer of and receptivity to friendship simply by shifting from formal to familiar pronouns or, as the literature now prefers, from "pronouns of power" to "pronouns of solidarity."[3] My sense is that this pronoun shift roughly maps onto the shift from mutual impersonal interactive accountability to mutual personal interactive accountability. Solidarity pronouns are likely to be used in prayer—in moments of being mutually accountable with God—and with children—for whose agentive welfare we thereby acknowledge accountability. The "solidarity" that familiar pronouns affirm purports to be a solidarity with a whole person, not simply with the project we are momentarily attending to. Pronouns of solidarity announce, or at last mimic the announcement of, personal accountability and a level of intimacy supportive of a personal relationship.

At various points in history, this distinction got co-opted for political purposes. Communities and societies have sometimes tried to impose the exclusive use of solidarity pronouns as a way of encouraging that level of accountability. For example, when the Religious Society of Friends sought to foster solidarity among its members (and through them to all humankind), they made "thou" standard in their nineteenth-century meetings, though by then the you/thou distinction had otherwise largely disappeared from English. With comparable intent, French revolutionaries mandated that the power pronoun, *vous*, be discarded in favor of *tu*, the better to foster *égalité*. These dictates mistakenly assumed that personal accountability can even develop, much less flourish, in the absence of personal acquaintance. The linguistic strategy of trying to import a fancifully richer, "revolutionary movement" significance into people's everyday interactions only had the effect of debasing the legitimate currency. Because real friendships require personal acquaintance, the mandate to proclaim them indiscriminately lacks full-faith-and-credit backing, so the usage drops out of circulation.

For friendship to take root and grow, it must grow naturally, drawing nourishment from a sense of widening agency and correlative personal enrichment. But though we befriend to grow and enrich our lives, friendship cannot take root in every soil. Many will last only for a season. Thus, the personal imperative is a blade with two edges, both tilling and reaping. It both prompts us to befriend when to do so promises flourishing, and it prompts us to withdraw when it no longer allows for that. If a relationship demands more of us than it promises, and if that deficiency cannot be fixed, we are obligated to disengage.

Marital Friendships

There is a particular kind of friendship regarding which the obligation to disengage has proven puzzling. Marital relationships have, or are expected to have, a unique quality that calls for special treatment as a social institution. Tying the knot and severing the tie are both legal maneuvers, so the conditions under which they can be executed are matters of public policy. Since we cannot regulate what we cannot define, gaining a consensus about what defines marriage is proving crucial. Here I think our account can be useful. It places marriage in the category of friendship, an agreement between two people to advance their stories as part of the same story. In taking vows, they each resolve to live in accord with the other's best interests: to flourish in one another's presence and to foster one another's flourishing. To "love, honor, and obey" is impossible apart from the mutual accountability that makes people friends.

The controversy concerns what sets marriages apart from other friendships. Traditionally, we have agreed that their intended permanence makes them unique. "'Til death do us part." Marriage is a life project. That much seems common sense. But it seems to raise a challenge for our account. How can we square the inviolability of the good-faith proviso and the life-project definition of marriage? Does the "'til death" vow leave room for a righteous divorce? Many argue that it cannot. If one makes a personal commitment to a life project, divorce can only be construed as a betrayal of one's vows. Betrayal is wrong. Therefore, marriages should be dissolved only if we can assign fault to one partner for breaking the vow.

In effect, such traditionalists are issuing this challenge to us: "Reconcile the commitment to a life project with the personal imperative to exit any relationship that no longer works for you. Otherwise, you must regard anyone who divorces, however personally justifiable that step may be, as guilty of breaking their vow and therefore at fault." That position regards "no-fault divorce" as a contradiction in terms. One critic described such divorces as "the abolition of marital obligation, and until they are repealed, Christians cannot say that there is a right of marriage in the US, for we do not have a right when it can be arbitrarily terminated without cause by the State."[4] Unless breaking the vows is someone's fault, marriage has lost its meaning as a life commitment.

The traditionalist view of marriage has long held sway in the Christian West, largely because its prototype is Christ's "marriage" to the church. Divorces in practice were sometimes accommodated with piously fraudulent conceits like "annulments," but breaking the vows explicitly was another matter. As they saw it, it could not be done without rending the moral fabric. What makes this view sound so reactionary to us is that, with the theological rationale having lost much of its social standing, we are freer to acknowledge the primacy of the imperative to flourish. It justifies divorce when there truly are "irreconcilable differences." But that does not answer the traditionalists' challenge. It does not explain how the primacy of the imperative squares with the marital promise "'til death."

Suppose now that we rethink the statement of resolve expressed in the vows, this time observing their temporal logic. The vows—the declarations of mutual resolve—were issued in good faith as a commitment to coordinate their lives to the end. But, like any project of resolve, their vows must be read for what they are: present statements of personal resolve. Given the fundamental function of projecting resolve, to resolve present intentions, the genuineness of the vows—their truth, if you will—is fully confirmed if both parties are acting in good faith when they take them. But keep in mind as well that the promise of a person is always a promise with the proviso that they can continue to honor it in good faith.

To construe persons as beings who can make irrevocable commitments is to construe them as de-centered from their presence. It is to forget that past and future are contexts for the meaning of the present. They shift and morph—we are all spin doctors—always aimed at sustaining a promising presence. If we assume a couple's maturity and good faith, their life project represents an investment in one another, each clothing their active life in the other's projects as well as their own. They expect their mutual investment to found stability and staying power. That makes it realistic to expect (as well as to hope) that their vows will never need to be broken. Nothing in this is a guarantee, however. We and our worlds are too fluid to pretend to irrevocable commitments.

The upshot is that the "'til death" clause is a necessary component of marital vows if they are to be sheltered by law. Two persons resolving themselves into one another for life announces itself as a unique kind of temporal creature, one that intends a body of movement, course-characterized by them both, extending to the end of their time. The fact that success in that venture is not guaranteed does not take away from its distinctive narrative character or from the distinctive richness and heightened sense of accomplishment it can work in people's lives. No comparable dimension of meaning and scope can be said of non-marital friendship.

Current Philosophies of Friendship

We have been looking at traditional ways of identifying friendship and marriage and at how identifying persons as characters of resolve can be useful in addressing some of the issues raised regarding them. Now we will look at some contemporary thinkers who approach the topic of friendship, which they usually do by defining the distinctive qualities of the relationship. On these, there is wide agreement: Friends love and care for one another, they enjoy a kind of intimacy, and they engage in shared activities.[5] As each of these qualities is considered, it raises issues that philosophers who discuss the topic divide over. From our perspective, these ongoing disputes only seem inevitable because they frame the issue as they do. Consider some ways we can sidestep their disputes.

1) Mutual caring. We care for our friends, presumably more than we care for those who are not our friends. Yet many ethicists regard such favoritism as a mark against us. They reason that everyone's well-being has an equal moral claim on us, since any favoritism disrespects the rational basis of assigning moral value. Strict Kantians and utilitarians oblige us to treat, respectively, all rational or all sentient beings with equal care. They challenge us to justify our caring preference if we do not.

Meeting that challenge is going to require us to show that practicing favoritism has greater personal value for us and to show that personal value is also moral value. The truth of the first claim is grounded in the fact that our mutual accountability bestows richness of presence on both agents far more than impersonal caring could. But the reasoning by which personally justifiable action is presumptively morally justified action is a part of the answer to the challenge I have to put off addressing until the chapter on moral value. For our present purpose—which is to hold our view up against the contemporary disputants on the issues—it is sufficient to focus on the personal value of caring and love between friends.

The word "love" is polysemantic. But in its most generic sense, we can think of it as the bestowal of meaning and agency on the life of another. "Friendship" designates a two-way loving relationship: Each party bestows a margin of agency on the other by merging their movement with their friend's, movement they determine in a character informed by their friend's resolve as well as in their own. In that formal sense, friendship amounts to a relationship of mutual love.

"Mutual caring" and "loving" raise tricky issues when we think about human agency in the standard ways. For one, "love" is a transitive verb. To love is to love someone (or something); that much seems linguistically fixed. That grammatical status, however, poses a question about the *ultimate* object of our love. Do we love our friend for our friend's sake or do we love our friend as an indirect way of loving ourself? What makes this question intriguing is that both answers seem defensible: We love our friends for their sake *and* for ours. Why then do some insist that the answer must be either/or and not both/and? Only because they assume—or at least follow the logic of the assumption—that persons have identity strictly as discrete agents. That makes them discrete targets for love. Either we love our friends first and foremost for the sake of making *our* life better or we love them first and foremost for the sake of making *their* lives better.

Forced to follow the grammar one way or the other, philosophers have taken sides. Some recognized the love of friends as unconditional in the sense that it is not conditioned on the value of the beloved. Many Christian theologians embraced this option. Thomas Aquinas, for one, found the unconditional love of a friend analogous to God's unconditional love for us, the idea being that God's unconditional love for us makes it possible for us to love others unconditionally. The other option—that self-love is what motivates love for friends—sounds more plausible to secular ears. But even they are likely to hear a tone of cynicism in that formulation. It suggests that loving a friend is a self-serving act at its core and that every friendship is one of convenience.

A third option, less appreciated in our time, is Aristotle's. He contended that self-love and love for a friend are compatible conditions. He could hold that view because his understanding of agency allowed for a person's interactive self-actualization in others. For instance, he insists in *Physics* that "[it] is not absurd that the actualization of one thing should be in another. Teaching is the activity of the person who can teach, yet the operation is performed on some patient—it is not cut adrift from a subject, but is of A on B."[6] Aristotle was conceptually equipped to hold (and we with him) that we actualize our life in the lives of our friends and they in ours. He even described friends' interactions as "procreative." Parents love their children because they procreated them, craftsmen prefer their products because they are their products, benefactors love their beneficiaries because they are their beneficiaries, and we love our friends because they are our friends. As parents put themselves into the child, craftsmen put themselves into their product, and benefactors put themselves into those they benefit, friends put themselves into one another.[7]

Aristotle deserves to be heard on this point, and if we apply what we have found about mutual permeability and the expansion and contraction in bodies of resolved movement, we can reclaim his insight. Because our acts of love enhance both friends, friendship as caring love can be solicitous of the requirements of each person's well-being without going against the requirements of either person's imperative. In friendship, self-love and love for the other are evoked with the same loving gesture of mutual edification.

2) Friends, it also is generally agreed, enjoy intimacy. They intimate things they withhold from other acquaintances. What is "intimacy?" Here

again, the model of personhood one assumes determines the parameters of one's answer. If one thinks of intimate friends as constituting two discrete sets of mental states, their relationship cannot be described as sharing. The standard models of individual agency allow us to imagine two people finding out a great deal about one another's mental states based on their behavior, but that only yields intense acquaintanceship. It does not allow for the co-creation of the mutual inclusiveness they enjoy in intimate moments. It allows them to be present *to* one another but not *with* one another.

On this issue too, Aristotle provides a helpful sounding board. He famously found it cogent to refer to a friend as "another self."[8] And why not? For him, one's virtues disclose one's form and proper function, which means they can inform two people in the same way. Inasmuch as he thought of persons as modes of active being, his "another self" language posed no problem. But in later centuries, when his thought was appropriated by thinkers who cast the identity of a person grammatically as that of an entity, his friend-as-another-self formulation started to sound puzzling and even off-putting. It suggested that two people who became friends really became identical selves. Montaigne's influential essay on friendship was pulled toward this reading. He lauds the unity of *wills* he enjoys with his friend: "I know not what quintessence. . . , having captured my entire will, brought it to plunge and be lost in mine with a like hunger, a like convergence, I may truly say, 'lost': neither of us reserved anything for ourselves—nothing was either his or mine."[9] We may blush a bit at the romantic sound of this, yet many of us have probably experienced moments that could be described like that. Moreover, if we transpose his "unity of wills" into our "unity of resolve" and "neither of us reserved anything for ourselves" into "both of us were as accountable to the other's life as to our own," the description can be voiced without tongue in cheek.

But Montaigne was heir to a tradition that defined friendship as the perfect union of souls,[10] and that led him to express his exuberance for it in a way that comes across now as cloying: "In the friendship I am speaking of, they mingle and blend so completely into one another, in so complete a mixture, that they efface the seam between them so it can no longer be found."[11] "Since everything between them is, in fact common—wills, thoughts, opinions, goods, wives, children, honor, and life—and since their harmony is but one soul in two bodies, according to Aristotle's very apt definition, they can neither lend nor give anything to one another."[12] Here Aristotle's "another self" language begins to sound overwrought, as though it denied lovers individual agency. It might even call to mind Dante's vision of Paulo and Francesca, suffering exquisitely in the second circle of hell, bound together forever because they let one intimate moment of shared lust determine their identity in eternity.

Contemporary discussions of intimacy no longer have Montaigne's metaphysical views to fall back on, so they try to account for intimate presence in terms of shared values, interests, goals, and sense of what is important. But, as Bennett Helm says in his discussion of this literature,[13] there is no consensus on what it means to share a value. Does it mean making the same choices or finding the same things enjoyable? Helm's challenge too seems rooted in the assumption that what friends share are categories of action. Intimacy might be based in sharing a fondness for eating Chinese food, enjoying gardening, or starting a family. This deserves its criticism too. Certainly, there are elements of a possible shared story in shared values—otherwise dating apps wouldn't work—but intimacy is only achieved when friends resolve their lives in ways that incorporate acting on those values.

3) It is generally agreed that friends do things together. We have seen that in doing things together—in interacting—we intentionally coordinate movements to achieve something we both want to happen. Each partner has latitude in how they advance that achievement. The choreography may not be well-defined. But there are parameters of acceptability, in effect guardrails erected by the conditions each friend needs to protect their own good faith. Because both are aware of moving in mutually supportive ways, they actualize each other in the margin of active being represented by the movement whose character they jointly determine. Accordingly, we should expect their time together to be more richly significant—"quality time"—and they should feel enhanced as an agent—"get more out of life."

The sense we have of how much a personal relationship adds to our life is perhaps most poignantly expressed by those who suffer its loss. When a widower says, "A part of me died when she died" or "I feel empty without her," he is telling the literal truth. A part of the body of movement actualizing his personhood did indeed fall aside; a part of his agency was canceled. We would also expect him to register that loss as one of meaning. Dr. Samuel Johnson, the eighteenth-century lexicographer and conversationalist, did that in reflecting on the effect his wife's death had on him. He wrote, "I have ever since seemed to myself broken off from mankind; a kind of solitary wanderer in the wild of life, without any direction, or fixed point of view: a gloomy gazer on the world to which I have little relation."[14]

So, yes, friends do things together. But the fact of doing things together is not a feature of friendship unless the character of what they do bears the personal stamp of both. Only then does the togetherness of friendship endow their action with the richest and most rewarding kind of relational meaning.

Multi-party interactive meaning

We have been exploring ways in which the actions of parties to an interaction, be it personal or impersonal, take on additional meaning commensurate with the body of additional movement they jointly intend. Sharing an intention makes bigger things (more movement-comprehensive things) happen, and that makes our interaction mean more to us. I illustrated shared intentions in order of increasing mutual involvement so that we could see how progressive richness and widening scope of involvement grow in tandem even on the impersonal level. Up to now, our examples have been drawn mostly from two-party interactions and relationships. But interactive relationships need not be dyadic. To better appreciate the scope of relational meaning, we need to take into account how the richness of an act's meaning and the body of meant achievement get co-determined in more populated interactions. Toward that end, let us imagine participating in different forms of interactivity in a variety of interactive settings.

Imagine first that you are in the audience at a Shakespeare performance. It's a first-rate cast, and you pay sustained attention to the "play" of action characterized by the actors' words and movements. Looked at by a third party, you might appear to be passively observing. You don't move much; you seem just to be taking it in. But that is far from true. Your active imagination is hard at work giving coherence to the play. Indeed, you are a connoisseur, someone who makes coherent sense of works of art with imaginative agility beyond what most in the audience can command.

The fifteen-year-old sitting behind you is paying attention to the play too, but she has little experience in following such a complicated plot. She is less practiced in discerning the interplay of intentional threads being woven into a contextual whole. Without having developed the necessary narrative dexterity, without having learned the vocabulary sufficiently, let alone the metaphorical nuances in the dialogue, and without being mature enough to appreciate the ways mature relationships play out in life, she is oblivious to much of the what is going on in the play. We can reasonably say that the performance "means less" to her.

In the same performing space, interaction of a different sort is taking place among audience members. You, sitting in your orchestra seat, are primarily interacting with the actors to achieve the play's meaning. But you are interacting with those around you in a different way. I do not just mean the odd remark to a person sitting next to you. I mean the intention you share with them in appreciating the significance of the actions on the stage. The fact that you share that intention makes your relationship interactive, but not interactive in the usual way, since it does not demand your attention. But because you all intend the character of the action onstage, you modulate your moves to accord with it—the expression on your face, even the way you are breathing—which makes you aware of an accord between your attention and that of those around you. If there is a distraction—like some idiot taking a phone call—it not only distracts (*dis-traction*—a *pulling-apart*) in the sense of pulling you apart from the play's action; it also pulls you apart from the unity you felt with the audience in attending to it. When there is no distraction and the compounded accord remains intact, the whole range of intentional movement—yours, the actors', and the audience's—are all ingredients in the play's action. In the moments of your collaborative success, the shared (in)tension is palpable. "You could hear a pin drop."

That impersonal layer of interactive significance is absent in the awareness of someone watching the performance on TV. She is intentionally imagining the action's coherence on stage in much the way you are in the theater. In fact, she even has some advantages over you: She can see the action from a variety of angles, and she isn't subject to distracting coughs and whispers. Yet at the theater you move in a field of imaginative achievement with both the audience and the cast. She interacts with neither.

For the actors, the performance is creative rather than recreative. They are creating conditions for attendees' recreative imagination. Moving in character, the actors intentionally lead the audience's imagination in projecting how they see the action playing out. Moving in character, they hope that the audience is "moved" by what they see. Not moved in the sense of "pushed," but moved in the sense of invited into interactivity.

In moments of success, the actors' actions' character expands to fill the house. To the extent they succeed, they can say, "It was a great house tonight." It is little wonder that actors who leave the stage for film or TV often return later to their "first love," the theater. Even if they are not paid as much, in the currency that counts most for them—the meaningfulness of what they do—they find it more rewarding.

Your role as connoisseur—generating meaning—is, as I said, recreative. But notice its distinctive structure in your awareness. You are paying rapt attention to the play's action, which means that you are not altering the way you watch and listen in accommodation to other parts of your intentional life. You maintain "aesthetic distance." If you did not, it would distort the play and deflect from the intention you share with those around you. Your attention is on the meaning of the actions on stage, how they present/represent the play's meaning. Ideally, there is no additional adverbial meaning to the action you characterize.

But this raises the same question we considered with reference to dreams. In light of the personal imperative, how can we justify giving over periods of activity divorced in significance from the agenda our life is organized around? The answer is comparable: The recreative imagining of an audience member, like that of a dreamer, can lay the ground for more fruitful creative imagining in the future. But, beyond that utility, there seems to be special personal utility in the case of the "fine arts." I remarked earlier about the apparent analogue between "works" of art working and the working we do in resolving our life. In the wholeness it aspires to, the resolution of a fine play's action intimates a *form* of wholeness we aspire to as a character of resolve. That can give it special resonance and sometimes even healing catharsis.

However vibrant the presence of interactive meaning may be in a theater, it remains an impersonal form of relational meaning. Are there also multi-party personal relations that give significance to our action? Some mission-directed organizations might qualify if their corporate intent is one in which all its members are personally invested and if many of those members are friends. That would enable them to foster a deep sense of community around their shared mission. For instance, a sports team intent on winning a championship might qualify, or a church, or an army unit on a mission behind enemy lines. In organizations like these, at least part of their members' interactive life has meaning in terms of personal relationships. That would widen their sense of the action advancing the mission. And if that mission is ongoing and doesn't end with the season or the battle, being party to an intentional community widens still further the accord they are part of and that therefore is part of them.

This set of illustrations seems to show the same pattern of correlated richness and scope of intended movement. Relational meaning on all these fronts and in all these modes represents ways we grow as persons and come to lead more meaningful lives. We are under an imperative to engage interactively for that reason.

Virtual Interactive Meaning

During the last few generations, we have continually innovated electronic ways to mediate our interactions. Now we have begun to fathom their enormous consequences both promising and threatening. Our struggles to understand and deal with these innovations psychologically, economically, educationally, environmentally, and politically increasingly occupy our public discourse. Let me end this chapter with a few suggestions of how our formal account of interaction might contribute to this vital discussion.

First, our account makes it reasonable to classify most of our electronically mediated interactions as impersonal. We buy and sell, make appointments, and deposit money, all without any knowledge of, concern for, or even belief in a person on the other end. This usually works to our advantage by decreasing the movement required to accomplish such tasks. We count it a personal boon when, by technologically augmenting impersonal interactivity, we "make time" to pursue other, more important projects.

The same cannot be said of people's attempts to mediate personal interactions electronically, and this is where I think our account can help make sense of the issues. So-called "social media" are sometimes touted as sites where people interact personally, but that claim is hyperbolic. Unmediated personal interactions make persons present with one another in their unique presence, their unique way of resolving their life in the present. When they mediate their togetherness electronically, that presence dissipates. How and why it dissipates has to do with what is involved in communicating personal meaning.

In high school, Jill had a close friend by the name of Jane. Jane lives halfway across the country now, and they haven't seen one another in five years. But they are online "friends," and they stay in touch by "liking" one another's posts and sometimes leaving a comment. Jill enjoys looking at pictures of Jane on a foreign trip with her husband, Dick; blowing out birthday cake candles; holding their newborn; or showing off their remodeled living room.

Consider how Jane's active life comes through to Jill in these pictures. In terms of our depiction of active awareness, each post presents her doing something with no adverbial import. It abstracts her action from its life context. Jill, of course, assumes that Jane is acting in narrative coherence with the Jane she once knew. Nevertheless, Jill is largely in the dark about the twists and turns Jane's story has taken. She can only vaguely imagine her "new life" with Dick. The presumption that now-Jane is narratively coherent with past-Jane gives her some purchase on continuing to claim to know Jane personally, but it's a purchase with a shelf-life. Little by little, the lack of renewed acquaintance renders obsolete her basis for knowing how to fall in step with Jane's life now. They have "a history" together and "go back a long time," and that history supplies a presumed personal context for the pixels they exchange. But because Jill is largely in the dark about how Jane is presently coordinating her life, her action is slowly drained of personal meaning for Jill, and with it, Jill's continuing basis for being personally present with Jane. Eventually, unless they renew their friendship "in person," the contextual meaning of Jane's presence becomes a mere construct, poised only on an assumed continuity with their shared past.

For most of us, this process of depersonalizing our relationships as we sustain them online is not particularly threatening. Partially depersonalized interactions with old friends are better than none. But again, most of us have established and now sustain other, unmediated friendships, and it is they that more likely supply the richest relational significance. The danger in the air is our sense of what happens when impersonalized interactions take up more of people's relational life than personal ones. The most social media–savvy among us, the young, increasingly interact online. When the pandemic precautions of 2020–2021 closed many schools, many adolescents who had only begun to find their way into genuine friendships were reduced to online relations that largely usurped their relational lives. When the school closures ended, they were reported to have felt exceedingly anxious at the prospect of returning to live classes and encounters. Having had fewer occasions for acquainting themselves with the character of another's coherence and having failed to practice that skill for a long while, they had to learn anew how to become personally acquainted and mutually accountable. Even before the educational hiatus, there is evidence that some teens and pre-teens who interacted on social media a great deal, particularly those most sensitive to social rejection, exhibited "classic symptoms of depression."[15] *De-pression* is an apt term for their condition, since agency shorn of personal relational meaning is *pressed down* as a volume of movement. Online, they were interacting without even being seen as persons.

Another way we are seeing mediated interactivity as an impediment to personal development is in the tendency toward prolonged adolescence. For the sake of convenience, we have been discussing individual and relational significance in successive chapters, and that may have left the impression that the ability to coordinate within oneself and the ability to coordinate with others develop in sequence. They do not; these abilities develop together. So it is reasonable to expect that a life starved of unmediated relationships would be deficient in the resources it needs to project individual coherence.

This serious downside to the electronic mediation of our interactive lives is real and deeply troubling. But we can take at least some solace from another affirmation implicit in our account. Electronic mediation may impede our active and interactive life by retarding our ability to dwell in the accordant meaning of others' actions, but it cannot remove our agentive impulse to do so, not if personal relationships really do enhance our sense of achievement and meaning. The quest for personal maturity can be deferred but not denied. Our natural proclivity as multi-intentioned agents is to struggle both toward character-rich individuality and character-rich relationships. Since the imperative to do so stems from the kind of agent we are, we are not doomed to live in a post-personal world. "Personhood" might seem like a spent signifier to a great many systematic thinkers, but in actual life it poses itself as an inevitable project.

3

Relative Importance

We have been distinguishing three layers of an act's personal significance: the achievement being attended to, the meaning implicit in any modifications the actor is making to the attended-to action, and the accord it has with the actor's overall agentive coordination. We saw how actions often have interactive significance, and how the same layers of significance—attentive, adverbial, and accordant—are ingredients in their character. Finally, in exploring the structure of a person's active awareness, we traced a correlation between how meaningful an action is and how much movement it intends.

Now we are going to explore another feature the personal meaning of action has, its relative importance. We are aware of an action's importance being calibrated with its richness of meaning. Our ordinary habits of speech bear this out. For example, we treat as rough equivalents statements like "It would mean a lot to me if you came home for dinner tonight" and "It's important to me that you come home for dinner tonight." That leads us to look for a three-way correlation—richness of meaning/scope of intended movement/degree of importance—operating in our deliberations about what to attend to next. Do we find that correlation? Does the importance of an action reflect both how meaningful it is and how much movement it intends? If it does, we stand to gain a new understanding of the personal decision-making process. Later in this chapter, we will see how accounting for personal importance this way supplements the standard accounts of practical reasoning to provide one that can factor in the personal meaning of what is being decided.

Let me emphasize here that *personal* importance in our terms is the importance an action has *in the moment of its doing*. That is a different kind of "importance" from what we ascribe to actions with far-reaching unintended consequences. (The officers' arrest of the Watergate burglars was the most important they'd ever made, since it led to the downfall of President Nixon.) The personal importance we are describing does not include unintended consequences. Rather, it is a measure of what we *mean* to be doing—attentively, adverbially, and accordantly.

Importance and the Personal Imperative

In the last two chapters we have seen some of the implications of being under an imperative mandated by our multi-intentioned agency, that being always to act in accord with the greatest achievement of our agenda. If this "personal imperative" is really the mainspring of our motivation as agents, we should expect to find our decisions about what to do next keyed to the course that promises to actualize us most. I am convinced that they do. To back up my conviction, let me point first to an ambiguity in how we use the word "important." We use it to refer both to the activity we attend to and the more movement-comprehensive achievements we are resolved upon.

Jack is doing a crossword puzzle. Jill calls from the other room, "Are you doing anything important?" "No, just a crossword puzzle." What Jack meant was that his puzzle solving didn't have anything in particular to do with anything else in his life. It was only meaningful in terms of itself. It had no adverbial content tying it to other agenda items. That made it an "idle" pastime, idle in that it didn't advance any of his more movement-comprehensive intentions.

Jill, in a wan attempt to turn the tables on Jack's earlier whimsey, called back, "What do you mean? You're working on a PhD in philosophy, aren't you?" Jack smiled and admitted that, yes, in that broader, present-continuing sense of his present action, he certainly was doing something important, important by the same standard that made his puzzle solving unimportant. Undertaking a PhD program involved a great deal of work and a great deal of accommodation on the part of other strands of his active life. What Jack was doing was unimportant only in terms of what he was attending to (the puzzle); it was important in terms of other present-continuing elements of his coordinated life.

I point this out lest our personal imperative sound like the imperative to become joyless puritans. We need not exclude spontaneity, serendipity, and frivolity from a life of obedience to the imperative because our overall success as a person is usually not threatened by attending to unimportant matters. As we saw in chapter 2, ranging widely, and even wildly, in what we pay attention to is justified by our confidence that if we should attend to something that threatens to counteract our best interests, "a little voice"—a little intrusion into our attention voiced by the accord we feel as an individualized actor—will alert us to that fact. In the absence of one, we are justified even in foolishness.

Jack, then, is not being disobedient in doing something as unimportant as the crossword puzzle, unless there was something more important on his agenda needing his attention. He would be guilty of disobedience if and only if his puzzle solving was, just then, working against his greatest actualization as a person. To get a better sense of how we draw that distinction, consider three conditions we can imagine Jack acting under.

Condition one: Jack has been pushing hard on various scholarly and non-scholarly fronts all day; now he finds himself losing concentration. He tells himself: Carrying on now would be a fruitless slog, whereas if I take time off I'll be more productive in the long run. Provided Jack isn't kidding himself, his puzzle solving promises to be in his best interest. It promises to be "recreational" in the sense of re-creating the conditions for carrying out his important intentions most efficiently. On those grounds, he justifies it as a good personal use of his time.

Condition two: Jack is in a good place. He has done all he needs to do for the day. It's Jill's night to cook, so he's got some uncommitted time. He's read the assigned poststructuralist essay and he's prepared for the logic class he'll teach tomorrow. All the items on his agenda seem to be moving along as projected, so doing the puzzle promises to add a small achievement to his intentional life, expanding his range of present accomplishment, albeit in a modest way.

Under this condition too, Jack's puzzle solving is recreational in the sense of being procreative of his greatest success. By taking his mind off his bigger projects and simply pouring himself into the puzzle, far from defeating important intentional undertakings, he continues to advance them as projected. Moreover, he stands to gain: Imaginative genius does some of its best work in downtime, when we're not paying attention. In fact, that's what just happened when Jill called him away from the puzzle. He'd been stuck on several clues and had almost given up. After their little repartee on the topic of importance, the answers he'd sought jumped right out at him. He'd been moving toward success in something he wasn't paying attention to.

Condition three: Jack's puzzle solving has no recreational value. He has spent the day following clickbait, doing crosswords, scrolling social media, and watching James Bond movies. Tomorrow he will be sitting in classes unprepared. If that's the case, then, in working on the puzzle he was, at least apparently, "wasting time"; his time was neither creatively nor recreationally engaged. Such moments of movement are neither important nor facilitative of what is important. We count them as "decadent" because we see them as decaying his agency. If Jack was being decadent, we'd worry that something was troubling him. We'd fear for him. If he went on indefinitely in wasting time, we could imagine him eventually unraveling and disintegrating as a character of resolve. In contrast to recreational activities of little intrinsic importance, decadent activities counteract a person's agenda. By defeating their resolve, they defeat them. Doing addictive drugs, for instance, often "undoes" people. Users sometimes slide from functioning well enough—maintaining a course of relative coherence—into abject dependency with resultant unsustainability as an individual coordinated life. One intention (to use) "consumes" them and draws them close to mono-intentionality. Their single satisfaction deactivates so many elements of their agenda that their whole life verges on being unimportant.

Thinking of our active life under these three conditions shows us when we can and cannot in good faith be spontaneous, silly, distracted, self-indulgent, or daydreaming. They show us when an active life flourishes in a carnival of possibilities and when it qualifies as decadent. Under all three conditions, the governance of the personal imperative in determining what is important to do seems confirmed.

Making Important Choices

I suggested earlier that by analyzing an action's personal importance in terms of the richness of its significance and the scope of its movement, we shed light on how we conduct personal practical reasoning. For practical reasoning to be personal, we would expect it to be guided by the imperative to actualize as much of our intentional life as we can. And that expectation would be met, as I turn now to showing. To illustrate how the imperative guides our conscious choices as an executive function, I want us to imagine several ordinary instances of decision-making as though they *were* governed that way and then to see whether describing them that way rings true.

Jack and Jill are now married with newly hung doctoral diplomas on the den wall. But they face questions about the next stage in their life. Jack hasn't had any luck getting a teaching job, while Jill has an offer from Big City University. With some apprehension they agree to pull up stakes and move. Both come from small towns, so there'll be jarring changes to live through, challenging adjustments to make, and important decisions to face. But they are full of hope. They see themselves "beginning a new chapter," one they will jointly write.

One evening they discuss what to do about the dogs, whether to take them along. They've been part of their lives since graduate school, so it would be painful to leave them behind. On the other hand, their new apartment building has no yard, so they'd have the daily inconvenience of taking them for more walks. That would mean curtailing other, more satisfying activities, so they would look on it as an "imposition on their time" and therefore a "downside." "This is not what I want to be doing, taking them down the elevator and walking six blocks to the dog park." Then, too, their new neighbors might turn unneighborly at the sound of the dogs barking. On top of all that, they'd have to pay a steeper damage deposit. Balanced against the advantage of their canine companionship, there are all those disadvantages that must be balanced against it, each, in effect, a sacrifice of agency.

How might they do such a balancing act? Presumably, if the imperative guides them, they would think of the advantages as richer time spent and the disadvantages as promises of impoverished time. Take the dog walking, for example. Jack never found it particularly satisfying in itself. It was a duty he discharged for the sake of keeping the pets healthy. But until now he'd been able to use the time to listen to a podcast or do a little bird-watching. Sometimes he'd ruminate on a paper he was writing. Every day he'd combine dog walking with more satisfying activities. In Big City, that looks less feasible. From what he's seen, neighborhood streets are too full of distractions to allow for serious thinking, too noisy for earbuds, and bereft of any birds but pigeons. The prospect of dog walking offers no satisfaction beyond discharging his duty to care for them. Compared to the dog walking he'd done before moving, he'd be diminished in how much of his intentional life he could hope to satisfy during the walk.

Risking moments of discord with new neighbors would amount to risking the breakdown of interactive healthy interactions with them, another kind of deactivation. As for the damage deposit, it would deplete their purchasing power, which also translates into a loss of agency: Purchasing power is the power to intend more because one has the wherewithal to accomplish more.

Against all these disadvantages stood that one huge advantage: If they gave the dogs away, they'd give away their companionship. Even canine agency allows for meaningful interactive presence, and any kind of interactive presence expands the sphere of movement being determined in character by their resolve. Let's imagine that their love for the dogs won the day and that they decide it is worth suffering the "trade-offs" to keep them.

We commonly refer to the reasoning we do leading up to moments of resolve as "deliberation" or "weighing the options." The advantages of keeping the dogs seemed to outweigh the disadvantages. How are we to understand this weighing? It is not, or at least not typically, calculative in the sense of reasoning with specific quantities. Corporate cost-benefit analysts may do that, but theirs is a technique for making impersonal judgments. The factors Jack and Jill considered had to be imagined in the narrative contexts of their lives. That made their awareness tacit rather than explicit. That being the case, it was not amenable to calculation. Yet they did have a sense of which course promised the more intention-satisfying movement, and on that basis they could make relative judgments.

Notice how the language they used (advantages over disadvantages) reflects just that comparison of movements. "Advantage" is from the French *avant*, "forward," as in forward movement, making a disadvantage an impediment to forward movement. Their relative judgment was that life would "go on" better for them with the dogs than without them.

Their next decision was whether to keep the car. Having it with them would provide the easiest way to get to Jack's parents' country home on weekends. On the other hand, renting garage space would take a sizable bite out of their budget, meaning that they wouldn't be able to enjoy eating out as often. Jill mulls over the pros and cons of life without a car. Then, suddenly, from out of the blue—from a level of her active awareness unattended to—the possibility of a better solution suggests itself: Maybe Jack's parents would be willing to ferry them, dogs and all, to and from the commuter rail station when they come for a visit. That would rid them of the biggest impediment to selling the car. Jack agrees to call his dad and raise the possibility. If Dad is willing, keeping the car wouldn't "make as much sense." In fact, the scales would tip and they'd resolve to sell it.

There is something about Jill's new idea that raises the resolution of the problem to a higher level of importance: It distributes the advantages and disadvantages more widely by involving more than Jack and Jill's good and that of the dogs. It involves the life of the parents as well. Granting the favor Jack is about to ask of his dad would have the effect of widening the body of movement included in the optimal resolution of the car issue. But, of course, then whether the solution is viable depends on whether the parents find its terms advantageous to them as well. After all, they too are under a personal imperative.

How might we imagine the parents deliberating whether to agree to the arrangement? Let's say that the idea initially appealed to them because they've always enjoyed the dogs. There'd be no difficulty picking them up from the station on Saturday mornings. But there is one snag, one unre- solved contention in the proposed resolution of things. Neither of them is confident driving at night, so they resolve to agree to the arrangement only if Jack and Jill are willing to take the afternoon train home. Short- ening their weekend together would be somewhat disappointing, but it seems the best overall arrangement under the circumstances. When Jack's dad offers to provide taxi service for daylight runs, Jack readily accepts. It's not ideal to have to go back early, but it solves (resolves) a lot of problems (contentions) nonetheless. "On balance, it's the best solution."

After things fell into place so well, it came as a letdown when Jack's dad called back a while later. He'd mentioned to a neighbor how glad he was that the kids would be bringing the dogs. "But the commuter train doesn't allow dogs," the neighbor informed him. That disappointing news put everything up for grabs again. Now they had to think it through again. If they sold the car and traveled by train, they'd have to board the dogs on weekends. Plus, the dogs couldn't enjoy the country, nor the parents the dogs. "I hate to say this, Jill, but I think we should reconsider selling the car."

Let me pause the drama for two paragraphs. We set out to test the descriptive power of the movement-meaning-importance correlation. Do the episodes we have related show that the options the agents chose were those most promising to achieve their ends and enrich their lives' meaning? And is it plausible to say that this promise made their decision compelling?

Think back to when Jack and Jill decided to keep the dogs. All the factors in their deliberation were directly dog related—the companionship they have with them, kennel expenses, the risk of alienating their neighbors, the increased damage deposit, and so forth. Similarly, when they made the decision to sell the car, it was on car-related considerations like parking expenses and ease of travel to the country. But then those piecemeal decisions required an imaginative resolution on a more movement-comprehensive scale, like the one Jill projected involving the parents' actions. When she drew the parents' movements into the body of action she imagined, Jack's request of his dad became a more important ask, more important because it was not only the best resolution to their lives but also drew the parents' lives into greater integration with theirs, thereby deepening the relational significance of their interactions.

The last two paragraphs broke the action of my little drama at a crisis point, so let me reward your tolerance by giving this story a happy ending. I do this to illustrate a third vector of importance, a third locus of movement that an act of resolve brings into being. In the first chapter, we explored how the character of people's resolve expands their realm of achievement—their agency—when they act in good faith and how it contracts that realm when they do not. In the second chapter, we saw how a person's agency can expand interactively, exponentially so in personal relationships. Now we acknowledge a third locus of movement determined in character by the character of our resolve, namely certain intention-satisfying movements in the lives of others who are not interactively present. We will call this the "legacy" meaning of our resolve.

When Jack's parents hear about the difficult choices their children face, an even bigger scheme suggests itself: "We could adopt the dogs! That way Jack and Jill can sell the car and still enjoy their pets when they come to visit. With the money they'll save on dog walkers and parking garages, they can easily hire a gig driver to get them to the evening train." After talking over the pros and cons, they decide to make the offer.

What might have tipped the scales for the parents? In the eyes of their children, it was a generous and kind thing to do, an altruistic act. But from the parents' perspective, it was more complex than that. First, there were self-regarding satisfactions in adopting the dogs. Not only were they animal lovers, but Dad was also determined to get more exercise, and taking care of the dogs promised the impetus he needed.

On the other side of the ledger, dogs take work, not all of it particularly satisfying. Then, too, they had never been responsible for dogs and would have some apprehension regarding the learning curve it would require. Those matters factored into the equation too. But there is another consideration that might well have tipped the balance, a legacy effect they meant to bestow in adopting the dogs. It was a gift to the children in that it opened active possibilities in their lives even when they weren't present with them. In intending it, they extended the character of their resolve into their children's lives and thereby expanded the range of their agency by the margin of intentional satisfaction the expansion is meant to make possible.

Recognizing this legacy dimension of our bearing as an agent—the way we can reach beyond our interactive life to procreate life in others—gives us a fresh take on understanding altruistic acts. For some, there is a problem posed by the word itself, "altruism." The benefit of an altruistic deed goes to *autrui*, somebody else, which they presume means that it does not benefit oneself. They presume that because they tend to anchor someone's intentional life in wants and needs, which are attributable only to individuals. That makes us the intended beneficiaries of our own altruistic behavior; there is no self-sacrifice involved. Mother Teresa must have wanted and needed to do what she did or she wouldn't have lived such a life of service.

The problem goes away once we see how we extend our agency in relationships and legacies as well in self-regarding acts. We can have both/and. An altruistic deed may be self-sacrificing in the sense that the person's individual projects may need to be curtailed, but that can be compensated for by enhanced agency on interactive and legacy registers.

The Logic of Practical Reasoning

I have been making the case that we have reasonable grounds for recognizing some actions as more important than others, reasonable by virtue of the correlation between an action's meaningfulness and the scope of movement it intends. This account of importance also complicates how it makes sense to understand practical reasoning. Standard accounts depict it as a process of finding the means to accomplish a given end. We start with an end and then figure out the means to reach it, or—to put it in our preferred language—we start with an intended achievement and then try to figure out what moves would achieve it. The model imposes a limitation from our perspective. It precludes the end from having adverbial or accordant significance. That makes the action we reason about impersonal in meaning. To accurately describe personal practical reasoning in important matters, we must describe it as means-ends (plural) in form.

Presumably, means-ends reasoning is not really reasoning unless it is possible to formalize some process of thinking that fits a means to multiple ends. To disclose the form of such reasoning, we might start by taking note of the temporal language we use when thinking about importance. We call especially important actions "momentous." Our usage reflects awareness of intentional movements as *moments* of movement. Our sense of relative moment, it would seem, is at play when we assess relative importance.

Before I go on to explore the logic of those assessments, let me emphasize that not all the practical reasoning people do is means-ends in form. Many of Jack and Jill's less important decisions can be described adequately in terms of means-end reasoning. For instance, when they decided to get rid of the car, they still intended to visit their parents. That called for determining a new means to do so. Arranging to go by train and have their parents pick them up at the station promised to be the best means to achieve their intention to visit the parents without a car.

But some of the other episodes of practical reasoning in our illustrations can only be described as means-ends in form. Take the deliberative process Jack's parents followed when they sought to resolve the dog dilemma by adopting them. They had multiple ends that they sought to advance; their solution provided an incentive for weekend visits, it gave Jack's father an excuse to exercise more, it promised amusement and companionship, and it meant opening possibilities in their children's lives. All these factored needed to be weighed together to outweigh the disadvantages they knew they were taking on.

Let me try to clarify this model of multi-intended practical reasoning by contrasting it with the one that Elizabeth Anscombe provides in her classic analysis of intentions. Anscombe unpacked an action's intentional meaning as a linear hierarchy of meanings that we can trace by asking a series of "Why" questions. She invites us to picture a man making up-and-down movements with his arm. Why? To operate a pump. Why? To replenish the household's water supply. Why? To poison the inhabitants. Why? To prevent bad people from seizing the reins of power. Why? To make it possible for good people to control the government and usher in the Kingdom of Heaven.[1]

Anscombe is not concerned with correlating the richness of an action's intentional significance with the amount of movement indicated by the answers to "Why?" Yet it is worth pointing out that her example largely bears it out. If the pumper had defaulted on answering the first question because he had no answer to why he was pumping—maybe he pumped for the sake of pumping, the way he sometimes drummed his fingers on a table or fidgeted with his hair—we would surmise that his pumping was of little importance to him. But he did have answers, a succession of them, and it seems fair to say that they tended to represent successively higher levels of importance, in terms of both more comprehensive bodies of intentional movement and greater richness of meaning. They "tended to," but perhaps not every one of them does. Replenishing the household water supply may not involve more than pumping, but it does involve as much. Poisoning the inhabitants (one "Why?" up) would *mean* taking additional steps beyond the pumping, like procuring the poison and measuring it out into the pumped water. Making it possible for good people to prevent bad people from seizing the reins of power would, presumably, involve many people's actions, many more than poisoning the household would. In sum, Anscombe's model of a hierarchy of intentions generally seems to reflect the three-way correlation—meaning, movement, and importance—that I am saying justifies our assessments of relative importance. That is not its shortcoming.

The problem (from our perspective) is that Anscombe's pumper, her exemplary intentional agent, is not portrayed as having a personal life. He had only that one goal, ushering in the Kingdom. The whole of his present intentional life was transparent to it. It is presently the ultimate "Why" of his life. A personal pumper would have a more complicated life than that. He might have a girlfriend who shares his political and religious agenda, and he might see their participation in the "movement" as a promising way to cement their relationship. He might also fancy himself a future Hemingway and be convinced that having revolutionary adventures will provide good material for his first novel. It is these enrichments to the character of his intent that must complicate Anscombe's model to personalize it. If it is not anomalous that Anscombe's levels of intention generally reflect levels of importance, we can be safe in assuming that each of the lateral hierarchies of intention in our personal pumper also represent hierarchies of importance. The various lateral intentional lines of answers to "Why" questions therefore multiply the meaning his pumping had for him.

I admitted earlier that assessing relative importance can only count as reasonable if we can formulate the process. In means-end reasoning, the formula is simple. We imagine the means that best achieves the end by comparing it with plausible alternatives. Anscombe's pumper presumably did that assessment for each of the graduated intentional frames of reference made by his "Why?" answers. But notice the shift in the kind of evidence he had for his assessments as the answers rise in their level of movement-comprehensiveness. He could imagine with some precision what movements would operate the pump and what additional movements it would take to poison the inhabitants. In fact, up to the point of "poisoning the inhabitants," he could imagine the range of movement he intended in an almost quantifiable way. He knew roughly how long he'd have to pump to replenish the water supply and roughly how much time it would take to buy the poison, hide it, and measure it out. Beyond that point on the scale of importance, things got vaguer. He couldn't project with anything close to precision the body of coordinated movement it would take to prevent bad people from seizing the reins of power. He could, however, judge with some confidence that it would involve a greater scope of action than poisoning the inhabitants did. Given his vivid eschatology, no doubt he also believed as an even greater field of movement would be needed to usher in the Kingdom.

My point here is that when we assess relative importance, we do not necessarily depend on quantifying movement, even in impersonal contexts. But we do depend on a sense of relative amounts of movement. The pumper can make *relative* judgments about the volume of intended movement his successive answers to "Why?" entail despite not being able to quantify many of them. Keep in mind though, to judge relative movement the pumper must assume that each of the higher levels of accomplishment he characterizes *has* actual specific volume, despite his inability to calculate it. He only needs to imagine each level of movement well enough to get a rough sense of that volume, a sense sufficient to making a reasonable relative assessment. In the context of his beliefs, the impersonal pumper can, for example, make a reasonable judgment that bringing in the Kingdom is his most movement-comprehensive achievement.

Is the personalized pumper reasonable in the same way that Anscombe's pumper is reasonable? If we assume that he can apply impersonal pumper-like means-end reasoning to each of his several objectives—furthering the political agenda, the relationship, and laying the basis for a novel—his personal reasoning can be said to depend on the same kind of discernment. Like his impersonal counterpart, the personal pumper has a sense of the relative importance of each item being served by his pumping.

There is, however, a crucial difference we also need to take into account. Anscombe's pumper can envision the full significance of his pumping just by rendering the early "Why?" answers transparent to the latter ones. He can understand the full import of his pumping because he characterizes it as a move in poisoning the household, and the poisoning a move in fighting off the bad guys, et cetera. The same cannot be said for our pumper-lover-writer. He can attend, one after the other, to his action's political-religious objective, to its relational significance, to its novelistic possibilities. But he cannot imagine in one explicit scheme the advances his pumping is making on all three fronts, not even vaguely. He cannot *attend* to it imaginatively as an intentional movement. But because he can attend to them serially, he can be tacitly aware of them as incorporated in the body of movement comprehended in his personal resolve. That tacit awareness is enough to ground his assessments of importance in reason. To act on them is to act reasonably.

There is one more crucial thing to note about our assessment of relative importance. We saw earlier that, since all movement takes time, we perceive the metric of importance as temporal. By sensing the moments of movement implicit in our action's meaning, its personal importance is present in their character. There is no clearer evidence of this than our use of the word "momentous" as a synonym for "important" and the way we refer to unimportant developments as being "of little moment." This linguistic connection of time with movement is no mere manner of speaking. The Latin root of "moment," after all, is *momentum*. But in the scientific era, the word got appropriated by the logic of causal reasoning and lost its sense of movement. In that role, a "moment" fixed an event (*e-vent*: *out-come*) *at a point* in time, a chronological point *at* which (instead of *in* which) the causal antecedents and conditions had the outcome they had. That kind of moment is a "portion of time too brief for its duration to be taken into account; a point of time, an instant" (*OED*), as in "The moment the light turned red, I was already halfway across the intersection," or "The moment I laid eyes on that gizmo, I knew I had to have one."

Describing our awareness of personal importance requires us to reappropriate the old sense of "moment," the one transparently deriving from *momentum*. Reminiscent of that original sense, the word refers to a volume of movement comprehended by how we characterize what we are doing or considering. To remind ourselves of this shift in temporal logic, I sometimes use that etymon, *momentum*, for our awareness of the temporal being of our agency. It better captures the sense we can have of "everything going my way," or being "stuck in a rut," or "suffering a setback." These turns of phrase give voice to our awareness of the volume implicit in the actions presently being advanced in our life. We define momentum in physics as velocity times mass; character logic defines *momentum* in a person as advancement along the course of personal resolve times volume of movement presently implicit in the character of that resolve. When an action adds to our *momentum,* its importance to us increases.

The process by which we assess importance is one we most often describe as "weighing." When we deliberate, we are said to weigh our options. We "ponder" the possibilities. It has always been so: The "liber" in "deliberate" means "scale." But notice the kind of scale being referred to here. All scales weigh things that have volume, but in either of two ways. Conventional scales, like those on the deli "counter," quantify the weight of a mass and read it out as a number. The scales we use to assess personal importance point to the course promising to actualize our greatest personal moment. That is a comparative judgment. It determines relative weight rather than a measure of weight. When we weigh our options, we weigh what we cannot always quantify. Like those of Libra, the goddess of justice depicted on courtroom seals, our scales of personal importance are calibrated to indicate preponderance.

To say that we can reasonably judge importance is to say that we can reasonably determine which among the various courses we think are open to us stands to *import* the most *momentum* into our life. Again, belief in the reasonableness of deliberation rests on two assumptions: First, that the body of our intended movement has volume, an assumption we found based in the fact that all actions represent a volume of intended movement. Second, that we can be aware of relative volumes in a way that establishes an order of importance, which we have just seen is reasonable. Since both assumptions are justified, we will assume going forward that all persons have a sense of *momentum* in their present life and that it informs their sense of the importance of what they do.

In summary, we have been testing a three-way correlation governing the personal meaning of an action—its personal importance, the range of movement it intends, and how meaningful it is. We have found that a series of explicit "Why?" answers is not sufficient to unpack the personal importance of what people intend in their lives, and we used that finding to describe how people make important decisions by gauging the personal importance of what they chose.

Important Days

To shed some light on relative personal importance from a slightly different direction, I want to consider now how our sense of an occasion's importance tends to vary according to where our gravity is distributed among the three vectors of vitality in which our resolve determines the character of action: in how we coordinate our individual life, in how we intend creatively into others' lives, and in how we create active possibilities in the lives of people who are not interactively present. Most of us find intentional satisfaction in all three ways of acting and interacting, but the balance among them is distinctively ours. The uniqueness of each of us stems not just from the worldly conditions under which we act but from the vector or vectors in which we are resolved to live most momentously. We each *create* a unique path forward, our self-defining way of directing life within the limits and opportunities afforded us.

To illustrate these vector variations, allow me to introduce some people, each of whom agrees to answer one-question questionnaire. "Name the day your think of as the most important. It can be a holiday, an anniversary, or a one-time occasion."

To imagine examples of people whose active life is pursued mostly along one vector is to generate stereotypes. Most of us, as I noted, distribute our investments of time and effort among all three vital fronts. But since we do not necessarily distribute our energies equally, I offer these admittedly stereotypical illustrations as descriptions of types of lives people live.

1) The first respondent is a child who names their birthday or other gift-giving holiday as most important day. Why might a kid think of a gift-giving occasion as especially important? Our account suggests that a big part of the appeal might be that gifts to a child often foster an enhancement of their agency. The gifts that delight them most are likely to be those that expand the scope of their achievement. With that tricycle under the tree comes a widened arena for acting and longer durations for projects. In effect, the best gifts boost the child's *momentum,* and that boost is what that gives the day its importance.

To grow in agency, a child must strengthen and enrich their active imagination. They do this when they play with toys that show them how to be bigger agents than they currently are. In this regard, it is interesting to notice that the way children expand their fields of action through toys has changed over time, interesting for what it reveals about the shifting function of toys. Roland Barthes observed that in the 1960s, giving children toys was meant to initiate them into the active roles they could aspire to play as adults. Little girls got baby dolls to "mother" and play stoves and ironing boards for doing household chores. Little boys got chemistry sets, fire trucks, microscopes, and dump trucks. Part of what has occasioned the change is the changing roles of adults and the changing nature of work. But I suspect that there is another factor at play. Electronic media have come to provide a scope of *virtual* agency that *appears* exponentially more momentous in the child's imagination than the job and home roles of yesteryear. Playing mom or dad was how 1960s children pretended to be grown-up, pre-tended, stretched into a presumed greater agency as a parent or wage earner before the fact. The roles a child is invited to assume today cannot be lived out in any actual—that is, non-virtual—world they can expect to live in. They are unrealistic. It is, of course, conceivable that there will be real-life analogies for the skills a hero in an alternative universe cultivates, but they are not, so far as I can tell, obvious.[2]

It doesn't matter whether the venue is virtual or real. Importance seems to attach to toys that widen the scopes of singularly satisfying intentions that they invite children to imagine. I find that a plausible reason for why the very young are likely to name gift-giving days as the most important.

2) We can imagine other respondents naming a day when some achievement of theirs came to fruition. It is the most important day because of the importance of the achievement. The respondent I am typecasting here regards it as a signature achievement largely because of how it commandeers a large body of their life over time. "The most important day was the day I passed the bar exam/gave birth to my first child/won a gold medal/became a citizen/was made CEO." Whatever volume of movement the day drew its significance from, its value anchored the day's meaning and determined its singular importance.

There have been times for many of us when we suffered a disarming confirmation of the connection between *momentum* and importance, times when the day's importance marks the achievement of something we have worked on for a long time. When it is finally accomplished, we find ourself surprised by how let down we feel. The temporal logic of agency tells us why: Having been accomplished, the celebrated achievement drops from our agenda. That letdown is an awareness of a sudden loss of *momentum*. Think of the "now what?" of recent college grads, a new mom's postpartum blues, or the restless early days of retirement. Having finished something important, we lose the hierarchy of actions and interactions around which we had organized its achievement. When it drops from our presence and no longer coordinates much of our life, we are temporarily diminished.

3) Imagine a respondent who calls Thanksgiving the most important day of the year. What sort of person comes to mind? I think of someone who celebrates the day as a "family occasion." Norman Rockwell's iconic, idealized depictions of family togetherness continue to reside in our imagination, so let me stereotype our respondent as the grandmother in the famous 1943 painting "Freedom from Want." Thanksgiving is important to her, I am imagining, because of the way it allows her to attend to her kinship web. In that matrix, she reigns for the day, if not as monarch at least as part of a matriarchy. We see her proudly bringing in the roasted turkey, presenting it to the three generations gathered around the table.

The men in the family are "familiar" too, but in a different way. In Rockwell's time, they might have been playing horseshoes; today it's easier to see them in the den watching football. Their familiarity is manifest in their easy repartee. The boys, their dads, and grandpa, Big City U fans all, show off their knowledge of player statistics or team history in a jocular way. For the most part, their attention is on the game, at least for as long as the game demands attention. They thoroughly enjoy their togetherness, but mostly as a sense of accordance that doesn't need their attention.

Not so in the kitchen. There, the women are paying a good bit of attention to family matters. Of course, they are also paying attention to preparing dinner, but only sporadically. It does not demand as much attention as the football game does of the men. That leaves them free to interact on a personal level, which is to say by attending to one another's lives in the personal presence they disclose. As we saw in chapter 2, personal presence becomes tenuous with the passage of time. After a year apart they have some "catching up" to do. Since they were last together, the life of each of them has been repopulated with a slew of new agenda items and the achievement or abandonment of others. Such reiterative phases have put blind spots in the character of personal presence they have with each other. They are all at a "different point in life," their personal stories having developed in new ways. Consequently, if they are to be present with one another attentively in a way that makes the day important, they are going to have to bring each other up to date. Only then can they know how the others are "getting along." Rockwell's Grandma as I am imagining her is someone whose interactions were richly personal enough to import great meaning and moment into their time together, enough to establish its superior importance to her.

With every approaching family holiday, we are reminded that the same accord that makes the day important relationally also makes its importance subject to threat. If family accord underwrites the importance of an occasion, family discord can cancel it. That is why advice columns are forever telling us how to handle divisive rants from Uncle Angry. They are never welcome, but they become especially demoralizing when the occasion is meant to celebrate and cement family ties. That accord can only be celebrated if it is restored. "That's enough, Uncle Angry. After all, it's Thanksgiving."

4) I want to stereotype the next questionnaire respondent as a US Army veteran in his nineties and imagine that he designates the D-Day 75th Anniversary Commemoration as his most important day in decades. He was one of the survivors who traveled back to the beach he once stormed and was an honored guest of the French nation. That occasion gave him one last time to be reunited with his fellow survivors. His heart was full. Like Thanksgiving for the women, the occasion had outsized relational importance. Long ago, their military training moved the center of his agency—at least for a time—from himself toward esprit de corps. As they regathered, he and his comrades not only remembered the Day in the sense of recalling it; they re-membered it in the sense of putting themselves back into their corps—the body of their interaction—into that organism in which and as which they had advanced D-Day's achievement together. In the present commemorative moment, they revived that continuing corps, albeit a diminishing one, and reclaimed their continuity with the historically active body they once vitalized.

There was another source for the day's importance to these men. Their actions and those of their fallen comrades were intended to save France for the French, which meant opening active possibilities in the lives of French people for generations to come. Those who came out to honor them were the intended future beneficiaries of their bravery back then. Most of the French people present were born long after the

Normandy landing, but they were grateful for the opportunities that the vets' resolve long ago made possible in their lives now. What meant so much to these men was not just the corps to which they belonged. It was the continuing legacy of their corporate intent. It was their bestowal of richness on the lives of future people. Both were implicit in the meaning of the moment and both fed into the importance of the occasion.

Each of these four illustrations of respondents is meant to highlight a life distinctively given to one or more of the vectors of important achievement—individual, relational, and legacy. They are meant to show how assessments of importance vary with the vectors of achievement most characteristic of a person's intentional life.

They show too that a day—even a Day—does not have the same importance to everyone. Some D-Day vets interviewed for a *Time* magazine piece reported that reliving the experience was more painful than fulfilling for them. "When we get together with the guys, no one talks about it. . . . There are things you just don't talk about." Another said, "It's something I'd rather forget; you'd have to be in the war to understand that. [Seeing] guys you trained with being shot up and killed, bodies and parts of bodies, right there on the beach. A lot of us wondered, What the heck are we doing over here? Why are we here?"[3] For these vets, reliving their part in storming the beaches not only did not *import* moment into reliving the occasion. It *exported* moment from their presence. They remember D-Day as deflating their agency interpersonally and perhaps even in terms of their legacy. Reliving the landing relived the decimation of the corps that had identified them; part of them died when their friends died. As for the legacy meaning of what they did, that too seemed to have exploded in their faces. "What the heck are we doing over here?"

What this second group of vets shows us is that there are crosscurrents of importance and exportance that necessarily make relative importance an individual assessment. It is likely that some who found the day too painful to relive nonetheless took a measure of solace in the gratitude of the French who lauded them, and just as surely, those who gathered all actively felt the loss of their fallen friends. There were tears of sadness as well as pride of achievement and joy in reunion, and each relived and remembered or renounced and forgot according to how the meaning of the moment either repleted or depleted his present life.

5) Finally, let us imagine someone naming as "the most important day" one or another holy day (or days). A holy day is a day of *ultimate*

importance for someone who grasps its significance as holy. It holds capstone status, ne plus ultra, on all three vectors of our intended movement—individual, relational, and legacy. To live in wholeness/holiness (cognate words in their Indo-European cradle) is to achieve perfect inner peace and perfect interactive health, and to advance a course of achievement comprehending the whole of the temporal order from creation to an end of time. To celebrate a holy day is to enjoy ultimate significance for what one does in all three ways. Yom Kippur, a pilgrimage to Mecca, and Easter Sunday all celebrate the perfect accord in a worshipper's intentional life, the unlimited reach of their relational significance, and, because their legacy has a part in newly characterizing the created order, the eternality in the moment their present life moves in. Each such respondent characterizes the day (or days) in terms of their own orthodoxy and legitimates its status as most important in their own distinctive terms for ultimacy. But they all celebrate the presence of a person whole in character, enveloped in a communion of common purpose, and advancing the movement toward a culminating accomplishment.

Imagine, for instance, a devout Muslim who submits to the five duties of every believer, one of which is to make a pilgrimage to Mecca sometime during his life if he can. In discharging that duty, he actualizes one of his person-centering imperatives, thereby being accomplished in more wholeness/holiness. The Hajj also represents an act of relational ultimacy in that those who pilgrim together take themselves to be bound in one spirit. When they walk seven times around the Ka'aba in the mosque, they do so as individuals equal in status and sacred in community (all, for instance, wearing the same kind of garment). Finally, their act also affirms and advances a sacred history that began in that place and is moving forward toward culmination.

Comparably, imagine a devout Christian woman celebrating Easter as a holy day by participating in the Eucharist. As an act of preparation, she asks for and receives forgiveness for her sins. What this interactive practice assumes about her active life is that she can bring unresolved ("wayward") elements of it to her attention and acknowledge that they defeated her wholeness when she acted on them. She knows that when she advances such discordant intentions—her sins—she momentarily disintegrates, precluding for the moment being the whole person she wants to be. Confessing her sins prepares her for the moment in the "service" when the celebrant proclaims forgiveness. This move in the Eucharistic celebration proclaims the good news that her intentional life can be made whole in character precisely by being forgiven her wayward intentions. If she accepts forgiveness, she accepts the gift of wholeness in God's sight, therewith the promise that she *can* regard herself as a whole person despite not always being one.

This act of making a person whole through forgiving is often represented in the Gospels as an act of healing ("heal," too, is cognate with "whole" and "holy"). To modern ears, healing stories—indeed, any tales of supernatural events—stretch credulity beyond the breaking point. At best, they are taken as "true" in a demythologized or symbolic sense. But skeptical thinking on this matter betrays an anachronism. Early monotheists lived in an era before the dichotomy between mental status and physical status began to reign over discussions of self-awareness. Since those channels were not yet flowing separately, awareness of being healed and awareness of being made whole ran together without confusion and became the powerful and persistent emblem for wholeness that it is.

Having confessed and having heard words of forgiveness, our Christian is prepared to move to the communion rail, where sharing the loaf and cup in an awareness of being one universal communion signifies ultimate relational meaning. Depending on the Eucharistic theology of her church, communal oneness derives either from ingesting bread that has become that body or, in the Reformed traditions, from sharing the bread as an emblem of their corporate life *as* the body of Christ. Either way, she is aware of acting in the unity of a whole communion, the "communion of saints." Finally, the celebrants understand themselves to be advancing God's Story, the Story of a partnership playing out in history, a history that began with creation and continues toward some version of consummated, resolved wholeness. In that framework of significance, the shared meal means not only feasting on present togetherness but foretasting the "heavenly banquet."

One final note about the possibility of a holy importance of such ritualized behavior. Our brief formal descriptions of holy day observances each presume a believer's willingness to act on the presumption that they can project their story as an episode in a divine story, the divine Personal Story if you will, since it represents the ultimate resolution of personal life. This is the leap of faith required, that one is obeying a personal calling and not indulging in wishful thinking. Of course, something akin to that leap is required for any personal commitment. Take befriending someone. It requires an act of faith, meaning an act predicated on believing that our greatest personal fulfillment lies with becoming accountable to that other person's story. Admittedly, leaping into a belief that one can interact in advancing a divine story seems problematic in ways that the rationality of belief in human friendships does not. Chapter 5 tries to diagnose that purported problem by examining how we confirm and disconfirm the truth of personal relations in general and how it can be reasonable to test the truth of religious stories.

In this chapter, we have looked at how a personal imperative is at work in determining what we attend to from moment to moment, and at why a *person's* practical reasoning is better described as means-ends in form. We have reflected on the different sources of an action's importance and how people determine it differently according to the way they balance the vitality vectors of their life project. In every part of this account, we have seen that no matter how a person resolves their course to make it coherent, the importance of their action is implicit in its character.

Emotional Force

In the previous chapter, we explored the temporal logic of "moment" as it pertains to action. The moment of an act differs from the moment of an event in having duration: It takes time to be achieved. We saw too that because we often project what we do to accommodate multiple intentions, we often mean to advance several agenda items in the same act. That means we are aware of our action's character as having volume as well as duration, and to draw attention to that voluminous nature of personal action I designated *momentum* as the measure of our sense of present achievement. Finally, we parsed how assessments of *momentum* steer our decision-making, in effect by determining the course most important for us to follow just then.

In this chapter, we are going to look at how our awareness of those ups and downs of *momentum* registers as emotions. A positive emotion is awareness of a gain and a negative emotion of loss. In addition to demonstrating that this formula is descriptively accurate, I show how useful it can be in solving some of the conundrums concerning emotions that philosophers argue about.

My approach here—finding emotion in the personal meaning of our action—will sound oxymoronic to anyone committed to contradistinguishing thoughts (which can be reasonable) from emotions (which can never be reasonable). Plato, for instance, invited us to think of ourself as a charioteer with two winged horses, one an emotional force and the other a force of reason, pulling in different directions. He saw it as our lifelong challenge to wrangle the irrational force into staying the course that reason sets.

While bifurcating thoughts and feelings has long been a go-to intellectual strategy for Westerners, when we try to describe intentional movement in its terms, we ignore the adverbial meanings that are required to make intentional movement personally meaningful. In real life, we perceive a mother speaking *tenderly* to her child, a college student waiting *anxiously* to see the dean, or a politician lashing out *angrily* at the press. We do not perceive the mother's speaking apart from her tenderness, or the student's waiting apart from his anxiety, or the politician's lashing apart from his anger.

This chapter looks at the way we read emotional meaning in the character of an action and at how our characterization of a change in *momentum* discloses both the force of an emotion (from mild chagrin to full-on rage) and its quality (like love, envy, glee, or boredom). Once we see how that intensity and quality manifest in an action's character, we see why its quality cannot be known apart from its force, and vice versa. Awareness of our changing personal *momentum* accounts for both. The greater the change we are aware of—be it an increase or decrease—the greater the intensity we feel. As for quality, that refers to how someone might summarize the narrative development informing their understanding of the expansion or contraction in agency. Since we can only grasp changes in *momentum* in narrative terms, our recourse is to identify archetypes of *momentum*-changing with whatever narrative types our culture provides (narratives of love, envy, anger, or boredom).

To get our footing for exploring the emotional dimension of personal meaning, I am going to describe a few ordinary emotional situations that I think illustrate my two contentions: that emotional force reflects a volumetric change in *momentum* and that the type of narrative contextualizing that change determines its quality. If thinking of emotions in this way proves descriptive, we will use it to rethink some of the prominent accounts of emotion that contemporary philosophers and others subscribe to.

Positive Emotion: Increased *Momentum*

A positive change in *momentum* has both volume (an amount of movement added to one's currently resolved-upon achievement) and a narrative context. As to the first attribute, think of the rapture of romantic love, the thrill of winning a lottery, or the gratitude one feels for a gift. It seems accurate to describe each as an agency boost. Rapture in love promises a burgeoning domain of interactivity, the thrill of winning the lottery promises expanded agency ("Wow! What I can do with this jackpot!"), and gratitude for a gift attaches to the active possibilities it promises to bestow, perhaps including the sealing of a relationship.

Evaluating whether positive emotions can be described as accelerations in *momentum* calls for looking carefully at a specific example of positive emotion. We have a long list of positive emotions to choose from, but the one that I think comes close to being generically positive is the one we call "enthusiasm." So let us adopt it for our case study. As the word indicates, the ancient Greeks took enthusiasm to be an infusion of vitality gifted by a god. In the *Iliad*, the gods enthuse their favorites with military might. In Euripides's "Bacchae," Dionysius enthuses his devotees with maniacal frenzy.

Enthusiasm is a good candidate for exemplifying positive emotion for another reason: It has long epitomized irrationality. After the sixteenth century, when the term passed into English, calling people "enthusiasts" was typically meant to depreciate them as unenlightened souls given to false inspiration instead of sober revelation through scripture, in other words given to emotion-driven rather than to reason-driven thinking. Happily, the word has largely lost that dismissive edge today. In fact, other than times when people break the ceiling of propriety and get "carried away," we generally applaud enthusiasm in others and are glad for it in ourselves.

Since an emotion derives its quality from a narrative context, we cannot illustrate enthusiasm generically. We must choose a type of enthusiasm to focus on. There are enthusiastic gamers, enthusiastic cancer researchers, enthusiastic partygoers, and enthusiastic jazz fans. There are also political enthusiasts, and it is they we will use to evaluate the *momentum*-intensity connection claim.

Political enthusiasm should be particularly worth thinking about, since the subject is both timely and puzzling. In some recent elections, it has mischievously eluded pollsters' measurements and surprised people with its strength or weakness. When polls point to a close race, pundits usually declare that the results will depend on turnout, which is to say they will depend on which voters are enthused enough to upset their regular schedule, brave the weather, and spend the time to cast a ballot.

Early in the campaign, Jill did not think much about politics. She intended to vote, but mostly because her parents had instilled it in her as a civic duty. Later when she started paying attention to political news, she noticed that one of the candidates (we will call him C) bore the standard of her parent's party. Filial duty then prompted in her a default intention to vote for C, but without much enthusiasm at first. As time went on, though, she learned that C came from a Greek family. Jill too is Greek. In fact, it's a big part of how she thinks of herself. The art on her walls, the fame of her baklava, her choice of Aristotle's *Rhetoric* as her dissertation topic, plus her volunteer work at the annual Greek street fair all testify to how much being Greek means to her. We would expect—would we not?—that this would make her more enthusiastic about voting for C. Why? Because she began to see her vote as identity affirming. Its added character—that of advancing her panhellenic agenda—made her more personally "invested" in his candidacy. She "put more of herself into" her intention to vote for C. The more she came to see voting as a way of moving other elements of her agenda, the more the act meant to her and the more important it was to her. Correlatively, by moving on several of her current projects, the prospect of voting signified greater *momentum* in her life, which is what she registered as greater enthusiasm.

Jill is a philosopher, so of course we would expect her to condition her support for C on his policies as well as his party and ethnicity. And sure enough, when she heard him talk about sustainability, inclusivity, climate change, and other causes she felt strongly about, it added to her determination to get him elected. These factors too tied the meaning of her support to agentive boosts. When C promised to introduce legislation to forgive a portion of student loans, she realized that it would give her more purchasing power, which translates into more active possibilities. She could do things that she has always wanted to do but, being a practical person, could never realistically intend to do. By making it possible to intend the satisfaction of more of her desires if C's policies are enacted, she stood to actualize herself more, to satisfy more of her intentions. This "more" imported more complexity into the meaning of her vote. It referred to more of what resolves her as a person, so, again, she felt more enthusiasm.

We can see from this perspective why political enthusiasm is so difficult to predict scientifically. By identifying voters with the categories they fit, demographic analysis filters out any multivalanced richness a vote's meaning might have by virtue of its significance in the voter's complex intentional life. In that way, algorithmic reasoning clouds over the disclosure of a vote's relative importance. Correlations of demographic data can approximate the relative strength of factors predicting the voter's choice, but they cannot grasp the storied ways those factors compound in determining its importance.

There is something else about enthusiasm that makes it hard to understand in the language of categories and causes: its contagiousness. Under the right conditions, it spreads through a community quickly, whether among Cubs fans, pop star fans, or rallygoers. Because we mostly hear the word "contagious" in medical contexts, it can prove misleading with reference to enthusiasm. Its transmission is unlike that of a disease. Contact is not enough; enthusiasm transmits only via a shared intention. It is only in sharing an intention that someone's agency compounds and enthusiasm grows.

Imagine Jill happening upon a public rally for C's opponent and stopping to take it in. Would she be likely to "catch" the crowd's enthusiasm? Not Jill. If she reacted emotionally at all to what she witnessed, it would likely be with anxiety or disdain. The reason she wouldn't "catch" the crowd's enthusiasm is that she did not share the political objectives that animated them. She was not disposed to move to achieve the intention shared with C's opponent and the other rallygoers. Without the disposition to interact, she would be "unmoved" by what she saw.

All this seems no more than common sense. But accounting conceptually for enthusiasm's contagiousness tends to defy common sense. Take, for example, this recent account by a philosopher of cognitive science: "Emotional contagion takes place when A feels an emotion and expresses it through an expressive signal, B perceives the signal and reproduces it, even automatically, that is, not necessarily at a high level of awareness and intentionality, and this causes B to feel an emotion that is similar or identical to A's."[1] The account not only overlooks how shared intentions condition contagiousness; it overlooks the impetus for enjoying the enthusiasm generated in sharing intentions. We can observe the attraction of boosting our sense of agency in all kinds of communities of shared intent. Baseball fans living in Boston tend to identify as Red Sox fans; in Toronto as Blue Jays fans. They become enthusiastic by making themselves part of a communal agenda, that of "boosting" their team. In boosting the team, they boost one another, their shared fandom enacting a momentary sense of corporate identity. They give direct expression to this awareness in their celebratory chant: "We won!"

Finally, a candidate can generate additional enthusiasm in voters by enlisting them in a legacy project. This implication of our account can be elusive for political candidates as well as for demographers. In a good campaign, voters come to see themselves as "part of history." Barack Obama promised leadership in "Change We Can Believe In"; Donald Trump, in the intention to "Make America Great Again." Those slogans signaled their respective political resolve by pointing, albeit only vaguely, to an arc of achievement projected as a new chapter in *our* national story. Participating in its achievement promises to add to the meaning of a citizen's vote even more than does their support for specific policy positions. Issues only obliquely engage people's legacy imagination. However vague a national narrative may be, it invites voters to imagine a momentous future and move in and toward its achievement by voting.

We have been imagining how Jill's political enthusiasm might grow along all three vectors of her personal being—by promising to enhance her individual life, by engaging her interactively, and by extending her personal reach into the future. By adding to the body of her resolute movement in those three ways, it seems reasonable to picture her multiplying her personal *momentum* and being aware of it as enthusiasm.

Negative Emotion: Decreased *Momentum*

Correlations run in both directions, so we can also be aware of diminishing active prospects. Momentary shrinkage in our active life is what we feel as negative emotion. You will recall that we adopted "enthusiasm" to illustrate positive emotion because it can register on all three vectors of human achievement. "Disappointment" will serve to illustrate negative emotion for the same reason. To be *disappointed* is to be *dis-appointed* from some achievement previously *appointed* by our resolve. When we suffer a breakdown on the highway, a power outage at dinnertime, a lost career opportunity, a loveless marriage, or a child who rejects our values, we experience it for what it is, a loss of agency. Something undertaken has been stymied; some part of our projected life has been canceled. When we are disappointed by some course of action, we feel "taken aback" or "brought up short."

Setbacks register on any or all vectors of intentional movement. All of them export moment from our present life. When Jill called Jack to tell him that something had come up and she could not get away for the weekend, Jack was doubly disappointed. He was deprived of *momentum* both in his individual life—he had been looking forward to the weekend as a recreational break from his job—and in his relational life—it would have been "quality time" with Jill. It would be a stretch if I tried to imagine the collapse of his weekend plans doing damage to his sense of personal legacy, so let us recall Jill's political disappointment to illustrate that vector. When candidate C unexpectedly got trounced in the election, Jill was "let down," largely because the movement she had meant to advance was now stopped in its tracks. The future she was resolved upon was no longer foreseeably her future, so it could no longer contribute to her present *momentum.*

Like enthusiasm, disappointment varies in intensity with how much change in *momentum* is happening or threatening to happen. Jack was more disappointed at Jill's news than he was yesterday when the ice cream shop was out of Rocky Road. Yesterday's moment of thwarted satisfaction was of very limited duration, and it had no bearing on the rest of his life. On the other hand, he was much less disappointed at Jill's news than he was when he found out that he had lost out on the only teaching job he had been interviewed for. That disappointment lasted for months. He had been projecting a career that seemed so rewarding. When no offer came, he felt "depressed" and "let down." Agentively speaking, that is exactly how he *was*.

When we compare positive and negative emotions, we find another difference instructive to highlight. An active moment of being aware of a boost to one's agency and an active moment of being aware of intending anew is the same moment. It is a moment of feeling "I can!" project a richer, more moment-comprehensive path forward. In contrast, being aware of a loss of *momentum* has, in that moment, negative valance, but how we react to that moment of loss/loss of *momentum* is yet to be determined. That is why it usually seems more appropriate to say that we act *in* joy (enjoy), lovingly (our love is in the act), and hopefully (in the hope that. . .) and to say that we act *out of* anger, *out of* envy, and *out of* fear. Love and hope are breathed into the meaning of the act and thereby expand agency. A negative emotion like anger sometimes but not always prompts what we call angry action.

There is no fixed and hard rule governing this usage, I grant. But that is because the distinction it preserves is rarely crucial in our reasoning. In moral reasoning, however, it can be crucial. Action done out of anger, jealously, or hate is open to appraisal as wise or foolish, or moral or immoral, but not the emotion that prompted it. Only acts can be judged, and it was not an act. It was a deactivation. That makes it a mistake to think that we are foolish, wrongheaded, or wicked in allowing ourselves to have negative emotions. The mistake is to assume that we could—or would reasonably want to—anesthetize our agentive awareness of negative changes in *momentum*. Let me try to illustrate this with anger.

Anger

Anger has a bad reputation among moralists for at least two reasons. The first stems from the Stoic contention that when we are angry, we are not seeing things rationally. The Roman philosopher Seneca went so far as to call anger a kind of madness. Since Stoics think of moral action as rational action, angry actions are seen as morally tainted by default. Their second argument is based on the premise that actions done out of anger always mean to cause harm. Since it is immoral to harm someone intentionally, anger has no place in the moral life.

Both arguments are flawed. Consider the Stoic line first. We can credit Seneca for distinguishing involuntary feelings from voluntary actions and for assigning moral value only to the latter. But Seneca was convinced that the irrationality of the involuntary phase so taints the voluntary phase that it makes it irrational as well. He held that the voluntary actions that we call angry manifest "a voluntary defect of the mind."[2]

Seneca was certainly right that involuntary anger is not the product of reasoning in the sense of deliberation. But he overlooked the sense in which the perception of diminished agency is the perception of an actual condition, namely one's own diminished personhood. Granted, perceptions can be unfounded. I might have misconstrued your words, in which case we would all agree that my anger was misplaced. But such cases are the exception. When we have our wits about us, we are normally adept at discerning when we are being intentionally diminished by others.

Aristotle appropriately called anger a response to a "slight" (*Rhetoric* 1178a31–32). He identified three forms it can take, "contempt, spite, and insolence" (1178b13–14). It is reasonable to read all three as deflations of agency. "[C]ontempt," he says, is what you feel "for what you consider unimportant." As we saw earlier, we gauge personal importance by the volume of moment imported into the character of the action we project, so when someone shows contempt for us, they are interacting with us as an agent of less moment than the character of our action has. Spite, Aristotle says, is "thwarting another man's wishes." Since our wishes largely reflect what we intend, being thwarted means being precluded from acting on them. As for insolence, Aristotle saw it displayed in the insulted person's shame. When we picture a person ashamed, we envision someone hanging their head, cowering, or otherwise presenting smallness. To look ashamed is to register diminished agency by shrinking one's physical presence.

Our agentive self-awareness of an involuntary feeling of anger is reasonable in the sense of reflecting our actual diminished state. So the wellspring of our anger is not necessarily polluted by madness at its source. Seneca had it wrong. Anger as a recognition of a change in *momentum* registers actual being. Whether it is reasonable to act angrily in response to the emotion, anger, is quite another matter. The question to be asked is "Does acting out of anger in this instance promise to optimize my *momentum?*" If it does, it counts as reasonable. When we picture angry actions like road rage, crimes of passion, and using foul language with the referee, and then try to imagine the likely outcome, it comes out looking bad for just about everyone. So let us give the Stoics this much: Most action done out of anger does more harm than good. But common sense tells us that there are examples of angry outbursts intended to be what the Dalai Lama called "healing anger." In fact, as Aristotle said, "A person who never gets angry when they are slighted or belittled is stupid and servile" (*Nicomachean Ethics*, 1126a).

Jack is angry. He's just discovered that Jill donated his favorite jacket to the homeless shelter. He had treasured it for the happy memories he attached to it, and he had fully intended to wear it until it fell apart. Now he feels "let down" at the thought that he can't. In giving it away without asking, Jill slighted him by failing to act accountably to what she should have presumed were his intentions in the matter, which as his spouse she was obliged to do. She thereby slighted their relationship as well, doing another vector of damage to his agency.

What if anything should Jack say or do? Presumably, a Stoic would advise him to brush the whole thing off. "Rather than letting anger determine your speech, calmly explain to Jill that in the future you'd prefer she ask before giving your things away." Now, suppose Jack takes this advice. "Please, Jill, in the future, ask me before giving any of my things away." One might best describe the illocutionary force of his utterance, devoid of any hint of anger, as a request. He is merely asking Jill to amend how she behaves in the future.

How might Angry Acting Jack confront Jill about the jacket? "Damn, Jill! How could you be so inconsiderate? I loved that jacket. I got it in a flea market in Katmandu, and every time I wore it, I thought back to that long, strange trip. What made you give it away? Don't ever, ever give anything of mine away without asking first!" Jill is chagrined. It had never occurred to her that he would even miss it. Now that she sees how much it meant to him, she realizes she'd acted inconsiderately. "Jack, I am so sorry! It was utterly thoughtless of me." Jack accepts her apology, and their relationship is solidified by the greater knowledge Jill has about his sensitivities and by the recommitment her apology makes to their mutual accountability.

Angry Jack has two personal advantages over Stoic Jack. First, he feels relief in "letting off steam" and in "getting it off his chest." These common ways we have of depicting it—as release and relief—are apt hydraulic metaphors. They reflect something of the infrastructure of agency. We are who we are in the character of what we are doing in the moment, and when that character is diminished in scope, something is happening to our agency. We are actually being slighted. So our anger is not simply an evolutionary response to a biological threat. It is an agent's response to a loss of active possibilities. It must be accredited as such, and Stoics cannot do so.

Second—and this is a moral advantage—in being overtly angry, Angry Acting Jack is being more forthcoming, in that sense more honest, in his relationship to Jill. By manifesting the exportance Jill's act occasioned, he is disclosing himself. What makes such transparency advantageous is that Jill thereby becomes better acquainted with him. She now has a more nuanced awareness of him as a person. She knows her own foibles better too; she cannot go on assuming men don't care about their old clothes just because her father did not. There's a good chance that this new knowledge will allow their relationship to run more smoothly.

We are assuming in all this that the intensity of Jack's anger is commensurate with the volume of the slight. True, we cannot always judge the authenticity of the intensity presented, but we do assume that there is an appropriate level. We find reason to worry when others hide their feelings from us and reason to get annoyed when they become "drama queens." Bodies of action have contours just as physical ones do, and we need to become aware of shifts in those contours if the dance of mutual intent is to be graceful.

If it is plausible to think that people sometimes use anger to maintain interactive equilibrium, it appears that the claim that anger by its nature is intentionally hurtful overgeneralizes. When Martha Nussbaum asserts that "anger involves, conceptually, a wish for things to go badly, somehow, for the offender," she certainly nods in the right direction, since most angry outbursts create an unhealthy interaction.[3] But if personal relations require the parties' ongoing attunement of their shared ways—a requirement imposed by the fluidity of our intentional lives—then it appears that expressions of anger need not always be intended to hurt. In our illustration, it was not Jack's intent to diminish Jill. It is true that he forced her to be actively aware of his loss by momentarily drawing her into his diminished agency. To make her feel his hurt, Jack had to be *sore* with her, and when she replied, "I'm so *sorry*," she was using that old expression to take on his hurt; she is sore with Jack's soreness. In that tiny episodic moment, he did indeed wish "things to go badly, somehow" for her, but only in a trivial sense. It is reasonable to image a wider characterization of Jack's outburst, one in which he is readjusting the terms of their relationship as a necessary move in the bigger project of keeping their relational life well calibrated.

Stoicism teaches us to ignore our *momentum* in making decisions. To do so is to ignore who we are. It is to ignore the feeling of agency as the site of personal meaning.

Emotion, Feeling, and Cognition

I have posited the expanding and contracting of agency as the basis for our emotional awareness. That repletion or depletion of personal *momentum* determines positive or negative emotion, and its extent determines its intensity. We have found examples of that correlation that seem to describe emotions more accurately than the standard languages of description. Now I want to claim an important philosophical advantage to this approach, one that deals with an issue prominent in philosophical discussions of emotion. My strategy, as usual, will be to make the issue evaporate by transposing the language in which it is framed.

The dispute I want to look at is concerned with whether emotions are caused by evaluative feelings or by evaluative judgments. Many philosophers regard the distinction as fundamental: A feeling is primitive—it has no parts—whereas a judgment has parts—like genus and difference, or subject and predicate. Our emotion must be prompted by either something primitive (like feeling cold) or something that has parts (like the judgment "There's a grizzly bear staring at us!").

What makes this issue so philosophically tantalizing is that we want to have it both ways. We feel emotion: Our chest heaves, our cheeks flush, our fear is palpable. But those feelings always have meaning: Our chest heaves as we sob for the loss of a friend, we flush in embarrassment for having blurted out a secret, and our palpable fear is connected to what we know it means when a grizzly stares at us. The underlying assumption is that the only way to allow for both sources is to formulate a hybrid account. But that involves a forbiddingly formidable problem. It involves bridging the Cartesian chasm, a feat that has long defied intellectual engineering.

Our account of emotions—as the awareness of changes in our personal *momentum*—avoids the "which causes which" problem by avoiding causal language altogether. As agents, we feel *momentum* because we *are momentum*. No causal bridge between us and our identity is needed. That makes an emotion simple like a feeling. Yet *momentum* only registers in a narrative context. That makes our awareness of it necessarily complex in character. We can conclude that when we think of persons as agents identified by the character of their resolve, their awareness of feelings and evaluative judgments are logical equivalents.

It may be that you are convinced by this dismissively brief brush-off of the evaluative judgment/evaluative feeling face-off. In that case, you may find the rest of this chapter unnecessary. But chances are, particularly if you are conversant with the issue, you have settled into one or the other of the two causal accounts. In that case, I owe you a more penetrating discussion of why causal accounts of either kind are unconvincing and, more importantly, why they are unnecessary. The prevailing assumption is that we must either say that our feeling causes us to have the quality of emotion attributed to us or say that the meaning we give to actions we evaluate causes us to feel the emotion we feel. I want to show why the *feelings cause judgments* view does not persuade many, and that while the *judgments cause feelings* view seems more plausible, it fails to account for how judgments provide (if you will) the "motion" in "emotion."

Consider first William James's attempt to site the cause of emotions in our primitive feelings, located in the physiology of our brain. What happens in there determines what we feel, including our emotions. "If we suppose its cortex to contain centers for the perception of changes in each special sense-organ, in each portion of the skin, in each muscle, each joint, and each viscus, and to contain absolutely nothing else, we still have a scheme perfectly capable of representing the process of the emotions."[4] Locating neural excitations as the substance of our emotions turns out to have awkward, counterintuitive implications. To his credit, James is not afraid to own up to them: "[W]e feel sorry because we cry, angry because we strike, afraid because we tremble, and [it's] not that we cry, strike, or tremble, because we are sorry, angry, or fearful."[5]

What seems right about James is his insistence on the primitive nature of our awareness of emotion. What we feel is what we are. The way to preserve that insistence is to transpose his language about physical feeling into language about feeling *momentum*. James's emotional feeling is primitive in the sense of being one with who we are. The same can be said of our agentive feeling of depletion or repletion. James's feeling is immediate because he conceives of his being physiologically. Our feeling of *momentum* is immediate because we identify ourself as the character of our *momentum*. By understanding the feeling of an emotion as a feeling of a change in *momentum*, we preserve the primitive immediacy of emotions without having to make such eyebrow-raising claims. Moreover, since *momentum* is only known in narrative contexts, we can preserve James's point about primitiveness without having to deny an emotion's cognitive content.

There are also combatants dug in on the other side of the Cartesian chasm. They hold that the judgments we make about an action's value determine our emotion concerning it. They admit that emotions have neurological correlates, but they hold with Robert Solomon that the correlates have nothing to do with the emotion itself.[6] In fact, one proponent of seeing emotions as judgments, Jerome Neu, provocatively called his book of essays *A Tear Is an Intellectual Thing*. Here, too, polarizing is problematizing, and the problem turns out to be every bit as awkward as James's. If we take emotions to be predicated on judgments, which are complex in form, then agents that cannot make evaluative judgments cannot have emotions. According to psychologist and animal researcher Frans de Waal, there are postmodern anthropologists who claim just that. They claim, for instance, that because emotions cannot be felt by animals without language, "it is impossible for people whose language lacks a word for *orgasm* to feel any sexual pleasure."[7]

If neither physical feeling nor evaluative judgment accounts of emotion seem free from problems, the obvious recourse is to draw up a theory of emotions that finds them sourced in both simple feelings and the "intellectual thing." But note the unexamined assumption here. As the matter is usually understood, such a hybrid account of emotions would have to be causal. Either our feelings cause our judgments or vice versa. Causation, one way or the other, must span the Cartesian chasm between feelings and cognition.

The "feeling causes judgments" option has proven difficult to get off the ground. It cannot avoid implying James's awkward claims. The other option seems to many the better bet. Unfortunately, it is only that, a bet. The cognitive scientists who hold the "judgments cause feeling" view are not oblivious to the mind-body problem; rather, they cite the newness of their field and express optimism that someday neurobiologists will discover the causal mechanism that explains how the transference from cognition to feeling happens. This is not so much an argument as the placeholder for one. Arguing on the presumption that someday we will have the needed explanation is asking for credit without collateral. It does not necessarily invalidate the argument, but it should be grounds for entertaining alternatives.

The only way to avoid settling for an IOU is to avoid depending on either causal link. I believe that our understanding of personal meaning allows us to do so. To demonstrate how, I am going to examine a specific cognitive-cause account that addresses what I think are the connections it needs to establish. It identifies a set of six beliefs that together, it claims, would cause an agent to have a certain emotion. My objective is to show that we can avoid making such causal claims if we transpose them, reading the six claims about the agent's beliefs as claims about the agent's intentions. That way, we find ourself able to preserve the force of the argument—which is to establish the source of emotions in the realm of meaning—without resorting to causal language.

The analysis I want to consider is that of Isabella Poggi, an Italian philosopher of cognitive science. I have chosen it partly because it provides a good foil for displaying the design of the non-causal account relating cognition and feeling and partly because the emotion it concerns is enthusiasm, which we discussed earlier. Following are the six beliefs that Poggi says jointly cause a person, whom she calls A, to be enthusiastic.[8]

Belief 1: A is pursuing goal G1.

Belief 2: A believes that G1 is a very important goal.

Belief 3: A believes that A has the resources necessary to achieve goal G1.

Belief 4: A feels responsible for the achievement of G1.

Belief 5: A believes with a high degree of certainty that A will achieve goal G1.

Belief 6: A has the goal G2 to pursue G1 with conviction, strength, and persistence.

For the most part, these sound like beliefs we would expect A to have if she were enthusiastic about the goal she was pursuing. For example, it is hard to imagine someone pursuing an unachievable or unimportant goal enthusiastically. But our concern is not with whether A would have these beliefs if she were enthusiastic, but rather with whether her beliefs are best thought of as *causing* her enthusiasm. To avoid making the causal claim, we transpose the six claims into ones about personal agency.

Characterization 1: A is advancing action with an intention characterized as C1.

Characterization 2: A's intention, C1, is very important.

Characterization 3: A's intention, C1, has been well deliberated.

Characterization 4: A's intention, C1, accords with A's personal resolve.

Characterization 5: A advances the accomplishment of C1 with a high degree of resolve.

Characterization 6: A is personally resolved in intending C1.

My strategy for undermining the perceived need for a causal account is to point out how each characterization determines the emotion without causing it. Let us consider each of the six transpositions in turn:

Belief 1: A is pursuing goal G1.

Characterization 1: A is advancing action with an intention characterized as C1.

One might assume that pursuing a goal, G1, and advancing the achievement of what one intends, C1, amount to the same thing. In many contexts we regard them that way. But a problem arises when we identify A's action in terms of its pursuit of a goal. It traps us into using the wrong logic of inference. When we identify someone's goal, we identify it using a *category* of action—like winning a game or paying off a mortgage—or identify it with a fact that relates categories of action—like "A will be named employee of the year" or "A will finish varnishing the floor by the weekend." As we have seen repeatedly, by excluding any adverbial meaning that C1 bears in A's awareness, our categorization of action ignores the contextualized active embeddedness of C1, embeddedness that discloses (not causes) its volume as a body of movement. That increase in volume is what A, the agent, feels as enthusiasm. Ergo, being implicit in C1, A's self-awareness of enthusiasm need not be accounted for causally by something outside itself.

Belief 2: A believes that G1 is a very important goal.

Characterization 2: A's intention, C1, is very important.

Recall that in our discussion of personal importance, we found it reasonable to measure importance in terms of the moments of movement intended. Comparable to what we saw with Belief 1, when we assign importance to a *goal*, that which is important, the goal, must be specified with a category, which, again, it cannot fully disclose in the moment informing A's assessment of G1's importance. One way to appreciate the difference between goal importance and act importance is to notice that the argument frames "important" as a belief A has about G1. That makes it a contingent fact about A rather than a logically necessary belief derived from G1's meaning. That contingency is what forces us to use causal language to link G1 to A's enthusiasm. In our transposed version, we assign importance to the active moment of A's intended accomplishment according to the volume of movement A intends. That sites the act's importance *in* the act rather than in something *about* it. If importance is implicit in the character of her act—in what she *means* to be doing—it is superfluous to talk about anything causing her to pursue C1 enthusiastically. Importance is *in* what A is doing, so it establishes her level of enthusiasm by implication.

Belief 3: A believes that A has the resources necessary to achieve goal G1.

Characterization 3: A's intention, C1, has been well deliberated.

A's Belief 3 is about herself, that she has what it takes to achieve G1. She has what Poggi calls "a sense of self-efficacy." It is worth pausing here to ask what kind of evidence might convince A of her self-efficacy with respect to G1. There are several possibilities. If her goal is to climb the Washington Monument, she might compare that feat with other strenuous things she has done successfully. Maybe last year she climbed up from the bottom of the Grand Canyon. That might convince her that she had the stamina and strength to climb the monument. "Yes, I believe I can achieve G1."

But this description of A's reasoning only applies in cases where G1 is a discrete goal. Since A's goal is truly important to her, presumably it is one around which she is organizing much of her active life. Suppose, for instance, that A is a horse-loving high school senior whose goal is to get an equine management degree in college. Does she have what it takes? Some of "what it takes" is meeting simple, impersonal factual conditions. (Does she have the financial means? Are her grades good enough?) But there are other, personal components of "what it takes," and assessing them requires deliberation. (Can she lead the social life she wants and still get up in time to feed her horse before classes? Will she be able to balance study time with dressage competitions and spring break plans with barn responsibilities?) Determinations like these call for her to consider possible trade-offs and then think through whether she can, *in good faith*, incorporate pursuing an equine degree into her projection of the most satisfying life. If she decides that she can, then according to how much she imagines the active possibilities this path promises to open, to that level she will be enthusiastic. Again, her enthusiasm is determined by the possibilities she sees opening, and those possibilities are intrinsic to the character of her course of resolve. Thus, we do not need a cause to account for her enthusiasm.

Belief 4: A feels responsible for the achievement of G1.

Characterization 4: A's intention, C1, advances the course of
A's personal resolve.

Belief 4 is that A's enthusiasm for G1 has, as one of its conditions, feeling (or believing that she feels?) responsible for achieving it. Poggi tells us that she is using the term "responsible" in an inclusive sense, "both [as] a notion of power and one of duty, with the former causing the latter." I take this to mean that A is responsible for pursuing G1 in two senses. First, the pursuit is hers. She owns up to having G1 as her goal. She takes responsibility for it being her goal. That being the case—given Belief 3—she believes she has the power it takes to achieve G1. Second, she is responsible for pursuing G1 in the duty sense of having an obligation to pursue G1. Poggi's reasoning seems to be that if A believed she had the power to attain G1 then, by virtue of it being her goal, it would become her duty to achieve it. But if this is the argument, it oversteps its premises. One could argue that if G1 is within A's power to do, and if G1 is her goal, she *will* pursue it. But that does not make it her *duty* to pursue it, not in the sense of being obligated to do it. Jill might reach for the corkscrew to open a bottle of retsina, her goal being to enjoy wine with dinner. If that is her goal, and she believes that she can achieve it, she is responsible in the sense that when she does it, it will be *her* act and *her* enjoyment. But it is hard to imagine her thinking that she was duty bound to drink the wine.

If there is, as I suspect, equivocation in this argument—agent responsibility as ownership with agent responsibility as duty—it may be a telling fallacy. We can think of it this way: If duty responsibility is not conceptually attached to power responsibility, there is no source for the dynamism characteristic of enthusiastic action. I suspect that the "motion" in "emotion" is being conceptually smuggled in at this border crossing, hidden in the trunk of "self-efficacy." Of course, it is still possible that her belief in her power is a factor in what motivates or activates her. It is still possible that, though none of those beliefs on its own works to engender enthusiasm, they jointly do. Accordingly, we should suspend judgment on the equivocation charge until we examine the cogency of the other two beliefs that are said to cause enthusiasm.

Notice how our transposition gives us a way around having to make A's belief in her responsibility the cause of her emotion. When we replace a claim about A's goal with one about her intention, the personal responsibility to achieve in both senses—ownership and duty—become implicit in the meaning of the intended achievement, provided it is resolved in her story. She is personally responsible in both senses for all and only the actions coordinated in her agenda. She owns C1 because it is an element in her resolve. That makes its meaning an episode in her personal story. And she has a duty to C1, since her story is in response to her personal imperative. We can hear ourselves acknowledging this root connection between responsibility and resolve when we say, with reference to some harmful act someone did *without* being resolved to do it, that they behaved "irresponsibly."

In recognizing personal responsibility as co-extensive with personal resolve, A's enthusiasm is determined non-causally by C1's meaning. The actions we feel personally responsible for are the ones integrated into who we are. Their character is translucent to the body of movement they are modified to accommodate. That makes their meaning translucent to the *momentum* determining the intensity of our enthusiasm.

> Belief 5: A believes with a high degree of certainty that A will achieve goal G1.

> Characterization 5: A moves to advance C1 with a high degree of resolve.

I doubt that it is descriptively accurate to ascribe Belief 5 to enthusiastic people generally. To be sure, it is hard to imagine someone claiming to be enthusiastic in doing something she did not think she could do. But it is easy to imagine someone enthusiastic about pursuing something she was not sure she could achieve. Think of all the writers in lonely garrets and all the painters in rented studios pouring themselves into what they hope will be a great novel or part of a prestigious gallery show. They know that luck usually rules the day in such matters, but they don't let that dampen their spirits. Or think of those movies about legendary underdog athletic teams playing for some high school state championship. Their members think they can win and they hope they will win, and they sure are enthused, but it would be delusional (and likely self-defeating) for them to have "a high degree of certainty" they will win.

There is also a question in my mind about how Belief 5 is related to Belief 3 (A's belief that she "has the resources necessary to achieve goal G1"). What does it add to her "sense of self-efficacy" to insist that she is *certain* she will achieve G1? I suspect that Poggi is addressing a challenge to any argument that tries to establish emotion (in this case enthusiasm) as a causal outcome of beliefs. Somewhere among those beliefs one must be shown to supply the motivation—the source of movement—for an emotion. A's belief in her resources is a belief in a fact about her. That makes it static, so presumably it cannot move her to action. For example, just now she believes that she has what it takes to get up out of her chair, but she does not do so. So A's *certainty* that she will achieve her goal seems to be offered to provide the dynamic emotion requires. The inference is comparable to the one in Belief 4, where confidence in her power (static) plus having the goal purports to create her sense of duty responsibility, a purportedly sufficient condition for the movement enthusiasm implies. It did not ring true then and it does not here. It suggests that A's certainty that she will achieve G1 necessarily makes her enthusiastic about the endeavor. In this case too, it seems the dynamic for A's pursuit of G1 is being sneaked in under the guise of another belief A has about herself. Once again, assuming the tenet of modern philosophy, beliefs are true or false, but they do not have relative intensity. As David Hume observed, "reason is perfectly inert, and can never either prevent or produce any action or affection."[9] So we still are owed an explanation of how emotions come to have intensity.

Our transposed claim—that her intention is highly resolved—accounts for intensity by definition. By modifying a great deal of her life to accommodate C1—our idea of being highly resolved in intending C1—she coordinates a great deal of her intentional life to achieve it. That is why we can say of an enthusiastic A that she is "putting a lot of herself into it."

> Belief 6: A has the goal G2 to pursue G1 with conviction, strength, and persistence.

> Characterization 6: A is personally resolved in intending C1.

The sixth and final causal belief put forth as the joint cause of A's enthusiasm is A's belief in a meta-goal, a goal to pursue the original goal in a certain way, "with conviction, strength, and persistence." It is not hard to read the addition of this belief to the other five as confirmation of the suspicions I have been raising, namely that G1's importance to A, her confidence in her abilities to reach it, her responsibility for achieving it, and her certainty of success in doing so *cannot*, on their own, motivate (that is, move) A in the way her "enthusiasm" requires. A could have Beliefs 1–5 but still pursue G1 unenthusiastically.

Picture A as the bugler at an old-style military camp. It is his job to climb the tower and play daily reveille at 6:00 a.m. Today he awakens as usual at 5:45, sees that it has been snowing heavily, curses, dresses, and trudges toward the tower. His goal, G1, is to arouse the camp. It is an important goal in that the life of the camp cannot start unless he achieves it. He knows he can achieve it, he is responsible for achieving it, and he's abundantly confident that he will achieve it. Yet we can easily picture him as decidedly unenthusiastic about the whole thing. That seems to be where the second-order goal (G2) come in. The claim is that if he sets as his goal to pursue the bugle detail with conviction, strength, and persistence, he will be enthused.

He decides to give it a try. He tells himself, "I'm going to discipline myself to start every morning with more conviction, strength of will, and persistence." Would we expect him to become genuinely enthusiastic just by setting those goals? It would be wonderous to behold but hard to imagine. He might bound out of bed determined to *behave* like enthusiastic people behave—with conviction, strength, and persistence. But it seems far-fetched to think that the feeling he generated by sheer willpower would be anything like the enthusiasm he would feel were he invited to play first trumpet in the Marine Band.

Once again, the long-recognized problem of trying to account for vitalization with a set of beliefs is unnecessary if we depict the actor's awareness as an awareness of acting. Conviction, strength, and persistence are typically characteristic of enthusiastic people, but not as additions to their belief system. They are *in* the character of their achieving. Consider:

What can it mean to have conviction? In the most basic sense, to have conviction is to have *a* conviction. It is to be convinced of something. In other words, it is to have a belief. In this case, it is a belief in G1. But, of course, that much was already stipulated as Belief 1. If all having "conviction" means is having a belief, A's conviction established in Belief 6 would be superfluous. There is, however, another sense of "acting with conviction" that Poggi seems to be capitalizing on here. People acting with great conviction are sometimes said to be "highly determined" to do what they do. But notice that being "highly determined" in the relevant sense is to be determined in the character of their action by the character of a great deal of their intentional life. Only this sense of "conviction" involves *momentum,* which, in the end, is what it takes to put motion in emotion. Conviction as belief has no *momentum.*

Belief 6 also posits G2 as a goal to pursue G1 with "strength." Again, if we think of A's pursuit as resolving her personally, her strength is implicit in its character. A's relative strength is the relative *momentum* with which she acts. She can be highly resolved in intending C1, meaning that a good bit of her intentional life is being brought to bear on its accomplishment. Or she can pursue C1 with very little resolve. When C1 is well resolved in A's personal life, its meaning is overdetermined by the richness of that greater body of action with which it is being coordinated. Herein lies her "strength of purpose."

Finally, Poggi claims that A's pursuit of G1 enthusiastically is caused by A having the belief that she is pursuing G1 "persistently." There is, to be sure, a connection between enthusiasm and persistence; if A abandoned her stamp collecting last year, it is most likely because she no longer had enthusiasm for it. But her loss of enthusiasm was not due to a failure to adopt the goal to persist. More likely, she lost enthusiasm because stamp collecting "didn't mean much" to her any more. It ceased to satisfy any intentions she had.

My objective in transposing Poggi's cognitive account of enthusiasm has been to show the advantage of thinking of emotions as the ways we register active awareness instead of as the products of our scheme of beliefs. I have tried to show why it is more fruitful to think of emotions as fluctuations in agency instead of as products of physiology or cognition. We have seen that by reasoning with the logic appropriate to characterizing actions, we can construe emotions as feelings of relative *momentum*. As such, they are meaningful in terms of the story they advance. Because the character of our action *bears momentum*, it bears emotional force; it does not cause that force. Emotions construed this way are intrinsic to our active life. They are indivisible from our action because they are embedded in its meaning for us.

5

Moral Value

Our account of personal meaning has been exploring the three vectors of personal agency—individuality, relationality, and legacy—each creating movement in the character of one's resolve. We found an action's relative importance reflected in the volume of movement it intends, and someone's awareness of that volume reflected in the *momentum* they sense in their agency. Then we went on to trace a person's emotional ups and downs in the waxing and waning of *momentum*. In all these features of meaningful agency—individual and relational significance, importance, and value as positive emotion—we found a pattern of compliance to a personal imperative, an imperative to enact as much of our intended life as we can imagine.

Given our recognition of this imperative to always do what most fully actualizes us, raising the issue of moral value would seem to pose a problem. If to maximize the body of movement accomplishing our resolve is the inherent obligation of us all, might not that obligation require us to be immoral at times? Might we not be occasionally obliged by our agentive nature to act at the expense of others? It is not hard to imagine a situation where exploiting someone—importing moment from them—say, by lying to them, cheating them, or maligning their reputation—might seem the most self-actualizing thing to do. Being "moral" according to the normal canons of morality would then be self-defeating and out of compliance with our personal imperative. True, people grow exponentially in healthy relationships, but why should we doubt that exploiting another might sometimes import more moment into our life than a healthy interaction would? Without a good answer to that question, we would have to admit that conventional moral tenets—to respect people, to tell them the truth, to be kind to them—would merit our obedience *only if they promised to edify us*. In that case, our account of moral value amounts to a kind of moral egoism, since nothing in what we have discovered about personal agency so far allows for any personal value other than self-interest.

The only possible defense against the egotism charge would be to have reason for believing that it is *inconceivable* for anyone's greatest self-actualization to require any unhealthy interaction. This chapter explores what it would take to establish that hypothesis. What evidence would give us reason to believe that a healthy interactive life is invariably the most edifying? With what evidence and by what reasoning might a person come to believe that healthy interactions are always more self-actualizing than unhealthy ones?

Early in this account we recognized that when we interact with others, we become accountable to them, and since grasping what accountability requires involves taking an imaginative leap, this process requires consecutive levels of imaginative prowess. It involves imagining whatever more momentous course of action they are coordinating with others to achieve. Only performing that imaginative feat can draw an extended field of movement into accord so that our joint accomplishment of that accord adds meaning and importance to both our lives.

The notion of a healthy interaction—one intended to benefit both parties—is going to figure in this account of how we determine what counts as a moral interaction. Provisionally, let me stipulate that moral interactions are all healthy. I realize that you may be inclined to think up apparent counter-examples to challenge my assumption. (For instance, a police officer arresting a criminal might seem to be working against the offender's interests.) Later in this chapter, in the section on Kantian ethics, we will see that counter-examples like this are only apparent.

If you are willing to keep an open mind on that topic for now, let me propose a new approach to defining moral value, one that traces the feats of imagination required in developing the capacity for healthy interactions. My strategy is this: If it turns out that we have rational grounds for verifying the personal value of each developmental step on the way to moral accountability, we should be able to discern the scope of moral accountability and the way we confirm its personal value for us.

How We Develop Moral Imagination

Starting early in childhood and extending into personal maturity, we achieve a progression of imaginative feats ending in an awareness of moral value. As we look back over the succession of them, we find we can describe each feat as an expansion both of our sense of agency and the scope of our accountability. In surveying that succession, I want us to take particular note of how we confirm the correlation between the scope of our agency and the scope of our accountability. That should point us to an account of both why we adopt a life of moral accountability and how we are confirmed or disconfirmed in that choice.

Surveying each developmental step calls for describing how we grew as agents from childhood to maturity by moving up a continuum of successively more sophisticated imaginative feats, feats that gave character to larger scopes of action and made us accountable for jointly advancing them. From elemental impersonal interactions, we graduated to personal interactions and to being loyal members of shared communities: With every step we enlarged the volume of intentional movement in which we were coordinated and to which we were accountable, and we found ourself edified by membership in that coordinated effort.

Again, the philosophical payoff I am attempting to win with these descriptions is a reasonable account of how it makes sense to confirm moral value, an account I then compare with the dominant alternatives: utility-based, duty-based, and virtue-based accounts of moral value.

To describe the graduated stages of personal development from infancy into maturity, we need to focus on four features they have in common. In each, (1) we imaginatively project a greater amount of movement (2) by accepting an invitation to widened accountability (3) in the context of an interactive relationship (4) that promises to increase our agency.

Stage one: Dad makes an airplane sound as he glides the spoon of pea mush through the air toward baby's mouth. Baby opens her mouth to receive the incoming. In effect, Dad is inviting her into an interactive dinnertime routine, and she is playing along. Why is she playing along? Beside the fact that she is hungry, she is playing along because in moving with Dad's interactive routine, she is moving in a more comprehensive body of action (hers and Dad's together), more comprehensive than just hers alone. By drawing herself into coordination with Dad's moves, the field of movement she (in part) intentionally determines increases her sense of achievement. Of course, this all depends on their cooperation. If Dad's a trickster and uses an empty spoon, or if he's clumsy and drops it on the floor, he cancels the interaction she was learning to coordinate with. If that happened, she might well register a total loss of agency. Infants are single-intentioned, so when that one intention is disappointed, in effect the *whole* of their agency collapses. "Breaking" into tears manifests her agentive disintegration. Happily, since Dad is neither trickster nor oaf, they do coordinate their movements. Fun is what babies feel when their single-intentioned life momentarily expands, which she registers by giggling.[1]

Stage two: Mom reads a bedtime story to her little boy, characterizing moments of extended movement by relating a series of actions with narrative coherence. The boy's fondness for stories is also related to his imperative to grow. In following a story's narrative extension of action, he widens what he can imagine doing. Stretching the range of movement he is able to project meaningfully strengthens his control over life. It nourishes the imaginative prowess against the time when he will outgrow childish ways and experiment with projecting individuality as a character of resolve. In reading stories to him now, Mom is bestowing on him a legacy of enhanced agency. More than that, their shared moments of following the story together are a matrix of relational meaning incorporating both their lives.

Invitations to interact are crucial to the early development of agency. We can see what happens when they are withheld. Heartbreaking evidence of a diminished capacity for interactive growth was on display in children raised in Romanian orphanages during the Ceaușescu years. They were tended by overworked functionaries who delivered food and other care with minimal contact. In the absence of even impersonal interactive presence, let alone personal presence, the children suffered long-lasting, often permanent limitations. Later in life, they were much less able than their age peers to form trusting relationships or enjoy a sense of self-worth.[2] Apparently, the capacity to love can only be engendered with love.

Stage three: We saw in the first chapter that when we pass into personal maturity, we become accountable for trying to integrate the whole of our active life, a calling we answer by projecting ourself as an individually resolved character of action, someone who intends to do things in a way that meshes with other things they mean to do. For most of us, it was our parents who issued the "invitation" to become an individual. They chided, reprimanded, praised, and rewarded us, in all their prodding, herding us on paths they thought might integrate our life most effectively. By being healthy themselves as well as healthy in their relationship with us, they modeled self-projection as an integral being. As we dwelled in their coherence, we too felt called to cohere. Finally, passing from adolescence into personal maturity—into the state that adds accordant to attentive and adverbial meaning—we enjoyed the agentive payoff of self-awareness as a body of movement greater in achievement than we had known before.

Stage four: In addition to learning to project our individuality with coherence and interacting cooperatively, most of us have come to make friends. Friends are felt to "belong" with one another, that ancient word reflecting our primitive sense of elongating ourself into a friend's life and being reciprocally so inhabited. Back in chapter 2, we depicted our friendships as beginning with an invitation, verbal or nonverbal, to take on mutual belonging and accountability. We found that the invitation to take on a life of being reciprocally respectful means resolving to coordinate one's life with the good-faith requirements of the other's personal project in every interaction.

This agentive move from impersonal interactivity into friendship calls for two imaginative leaps beyond those required for impersonal interactions. First, would-be friends must have some sense of how the other's life coheres. At first, limited episodes made for only a sketchy coherence. Then, as they perceive more moments of each other's coordination, a richer coherence emerges. The more extensive imaginative leap needed to befriend someone is that of projecting life in accord with them. Both friends must find it plausible to believe that they can, in good faith, resolve their two stories as they presently project them.

When I illustrated the earlier stages along life's agentive way, the invitations and acceptances were evident: Dad's spoon invitation and baby's acceptance, Mom's "once upon a time" and son's rapt attention, parents' encouragements and admonishments and their child's compliance (or not). In the case of making friends, the invitations to belonging and accountability are often offered tacitly and accepted tacitly. But I believe they do take place in a process of "reaching an understanding" of their relationship as a friendship.

The terms of that relationship usually are only made explicit when couples exchange wedding vows. "Do you promise?" "I do." The terms need to be explicit because the record of a marriage is a public legal one. Informal friendships are more likely to be achieved when one party begins to act with apparent personal accountability to the other. They may act solicitously regarding the other's wider agenda. Such "friendly" gestures are then either reciprocated or not. Reciprocation may simply be by following suit, moving in step with the friendly treatment. That alone may be enough to affirm a mutual understanding, particularly if it is affirmed and reaffirmed even under stress, when you "find out who your real friends are." If friends remain "true" to one another—continuing to interact to the greatest actualization of both—they bestow meaning and moment on each other's life, so confirming to both the value of their relationship.

Stage five: It may be tempting to suppose that we have already arrived at a satisfactory definition of the moral life, that being a life of love and loyalty. But that stage four level of accountability—to the good of those we love—is too narrow to define moral obligation. At a minimum, moral obligations also extend to members of the broader communities of shared intentions to which we "belong." We join them because they make possible accomplishing more of what we intend. In sync with various group and civil norms, our way is made smoother so that we maintain our projects with greater *momentum.* Here, too, we observe how it can be agentively advantageous to coordinate with various communities of shared intention, and that advantage underwrites the obligation to do so. This leads us to value laws and customs that foster healthy interactions and benefit everyone coordinated by them.

When we broaden our account of the scope of moral obligation to include the web of communal affiliations we enjoy, we certainly move in the right direction, since we are moving toward greater self-actualization. In fact, many people define moral obligation just that way, as the duty to maintain only healthy interactivity within their various ingroups. The ancient Greek word for the obligations that define group-accountability is *mores,* the values of one's community. Since that word is the source of "morals," communal or cultural norms would seem to have defined moral obligation for a very long time.

But this relic of our intellectual heritage proves too limiting as well. Perhaps we can see this best if we take note of how the common features of meaning/movement/moment extension apply here. We form mores obligations when we identify with a group: We become an "us" and we become accountable to our communal success by fostering healthy interactions among "us." Mores communities, having multiple members, often find it expedient to avoid misunderstandings by making the conditions of membership—invitation and acceptance—explicit. Unlike the tacit inviting and accepting that go on in forming casual friendships, invitations to join mores communities are more like marriage ceremonies. The rituals of reciprocity are often explicitly extended and accepted. A candidate is offered membership—recruited by the Marine Corps, tapped by a sorority, hired by a brokerage firm, introduced into a street gang, told she has made the team—then informed of the scope of their new accountability—in boot camp, in rights of initiation, in the advice of a mentor, in blood oaths, in lectures by the coach—then made to demonstrate fealty to those terms—by surviving boot camp, sitting with the group in the dining hall, showing loyalty to the firm, defending the gang's turf, or manifesting a good attitude on the field. The payoff, when there is one, is to feel bigger than oneself, to be incorporated into a body of action whose character one is co-characterizing and whose agency one is co-actualizing.

As we noted earlier—and this is the crucial distinction we need to refine—genuine morality represents accountability to a greater body of accord than is defined by any communal in-group. In some sense, it is must be "universal." But in what sense? Our question, then: How does our account of personal meaning determine the specific reach of a person's moral accountability?

Given that healthy interactions require mutual commitment, one limit to that reach becomes apparent upon reflection. We cannot aspire to have a healthy interactive relationship with everyone we meet. With most people, there are no mutually advantageous interactions in prospect. We don't "have anything in common." Also, there are people who, if we interacted with them, would mean to exploit us. With much of the social world going on around us being irrelevant to our purposes or counterproductive of them, interacting in those social situations could not be something we are personally obliged to do. If we exclude those whom we have no occasion to interact with and those who intend us harm, we are left with a sphere of moral obligation including all good-willed people we chose to interact with. Our moral obligation is to intend only healthy interactions with them.

I suggested earlier that each successive stage in the development of moral imagination, as was the case at each earlier stage, involves a more formidable imaginative feat. One must grasp a greater scope of coordinated movement to be able to project one's action to advance it. That leaves us with the question of how it is possible to imagine the coordinated body of life that defines the scope and nature of moral accountability.

In our examples of the in-groups that provide our mores memberships, we were typically able to exemplify the mores explicitly, like the pledges of allegiance to be recited, employee handbooks to be consulted, coaches' lectures to be suffered, and mentors to be heeded. In each case, we had a good idea of what coordinated body of movement we were signed up to advance. Here, on the most comprehensive of all levels of personal accountability, I believe we are forced to choose between two ways of representing the universal community of good-willed people, a personal way or an impersonal way.

In modernity, by default, systematic rational thinkers try to define moral value impersonally. I am thinking here of philosophers like Mill, Kant, and Aristotle, all of whom reason about right and wrong with categories of action. The other option, to personalize moral value, is built on seeing coherent personal character in the body of action we are accountable to. Those who conceptualize moral value depersonalize it; those who personalize moral value display it in narratives. The gulf between these two ways of imagining the scope of accountability is unbridgeable because of the different logics of inference each uses to understand action. Whichever method we choose "stands to reason" for us.

Jill is a good-willed person. She tries to have mutually beneficial interactions with everyone she meets whenever she can. She is determined never to exploit anyone by achieving her intentions at their expense. When she does run into someone she thinks will take advantage of her, she avoids them if she can.

Jill, being an observant person, knows that not everyone goes through life disposed this way, so she can't help but wonder why she is the good-willed person she is. How might she justify her moral stance? As someone who has studied philosophical ethics, she may be inclined to frame her options as alternative sets of explicit criteria for assigning moral value. She has read Mill and Kant, so she might frame her accountability as obedience to a rule like "Always act to maximize happiness" or "Always act in obedience to the categorical imperative." Given her professional proclivities, we wouldn't be surprised to find Jill adopting such a rule to define her conceptual hold on what she is morally accountable for doing.

Then again, maybe she, along with us, has been exploring a character-of-resolve account of personal meaning and finds herself open to looking at moral reasoning as narratively contextualized. She would then begin to think of universal moral community (UMC) in terms of an ongoing storyline being advanced by all persons interacting with good-will. Instead of specifying UMC as those who follow the right conceptual formula for right conduct, she would imagine it as *personal* in form, the resolution of a coordinated body of good-willed intentional life. If persons in a universal community of the good-willed can be resolved with one another in practice, their resolution characterizes a coherent course of action that qualifies as a personal story.

As our way to distinguish this "person" who incarnates all good-willed people, I use Person, indicating with the uppercase *P* that it is a person with a resolution of personal actions than which no more comprehensive resolution can be conceived. It is a person who incorporates the lives of all those resolved to live in UMC.

By this point, you have probably identified the historical prototypes for narratives of personal character I am putting forth as sources of moral meaning. The paradigm for what guarantees genuine, universal, non-*mores*-limited moral meaning has been provided in the West by the Stories of the Abrahamic monotheisms. They tell of a Personal God inviting human persons into widened covenantal accountability and, in the same divine act, bestowing on them the gift of abundant life. God invites or "calls" (Israel, the church, the followers of the Prophet) to be accountable to others (in promoting justice, feeding the poor). The peoples called received their calling as a "blessing," which is to say as a gift of living a new life, even of being a "new creation." It binds them in a covenant community of the "called."

Admittedly, the ancient monotheisms did not initially tell Stories of universal moral accountability. It took generations of retellings before the Storytellers escaped their tribal mentalities and got beyond parochialism. But by the eighth century BCE, Judaism had come to see itself as "a light to the nations," and by early in the Christian era the Church had embraced Gentile members. Those moves into universality made moral accountability universal in the sense of applying to *all* people of goodwill.

How might Jill go about deciding which logical route to take in assigning moral value? Let's say that she has no religious affiliation and affirms no religious beliefs, but that she stands open to taking seriously the character logic basis for moral value. That puts her in an odd epistemic place. On the one hand, she finds it plausible to identify persons as characters of resolve, and she believes that characters of resolve can form communities of accord; on the other hand, she has no grounds for believing in UMC as the truth of an inherited Personal Story.

The Secular Passage from *Mores*-Morals to UMC-Based Morals

For our personalist-curious Jill, the question becomes, what should she look for to confirm or disconfirm the truth of UMC? She thinks back through the agentive stages of her development, noting how each successive imaginative feat was both more comprehensive in the range of accordance it held itself accountable to and more advantaged by the margin of *momentum* it promised. She notes as well that each graduated stage of her agentive development was confirmed or disconfirmed as truly dependable—as faithful to the "troth" pledge—according to whether her wider accountability was being rewarded with a greater sense of agency. For as long as she was agentively advantaged—given additional *momentum*—by taking on that broader accountability, the relationship was held to be true. Given that pattern, how might we expect her to be invited into UMC, and how might we expect her to decide whether acting in that belief added meaning and moment to her life?

The invitation—analogous to that of Dad to baby, Mom to son, friend to friend—would have to be to engage in only healthy interactions *across mores boundaries*. In the world religions that function as dominant historical vehicles for Western reasoning about UMC, iconic figures are represented as doing just that: Jesus showing accountability to Samaritans, Paul to Gentile converts, Gandhi preaching accord between Hindus and Muslims, and the Revs. Martin Luther King and Bishop Desmond Tutu championing multiracial societies. They beckoned people to a promised land of accord beyond tribe. They promised their followers that acting in personal solidarity with UMC would incorporate them into the greatest conceivable healthy body of action and give them the greatest conceivable *momentum*.

Confirmation of UMC could only come after accepting the invitation to join. That is part of what is meant in recognizing that faith is the source of belief. It would confirm itself as personal relationships all do, by proving fruitful in meaning and moment over continuing interactions. And that "troth" would be disconfirmed in our eyes if we were unable to live to the fullest without exploiting others or they us. Either eventuality would disconfirm UMC and with it any universal basis for moral value.

If, as I have suggested, understanding persons as characters of resolve leads us to Personify UMC, the tie between belief in God and belief in moral value is implicit in a personalism based in the logic of agency. That makes belief in UMC reasonable in two senses. First, it is intelligible.

There is nothing incoherent in thinking of an ongoing project resolving the actions of all good-willed people. Second, it is subject to confirmation and disconfirmation. It is confirmed whenever we interact with other good-willed people and find fulfilment in each other's interactive presence even across our cultural differences. It would be disconfirmed were we to find ourself having to exploit another to maintain our own good faith, or another having to exploit us to maintain theirs. Either disconfirmation would give credence to moral cynicism, the belief that personal good and moral good can be at odds, and that when they are at odds the personal imperative takes precedence. If UMC is discredited, mores solidarity has status as the highest source of personal value we can appeal to.

On the other hand, someone who affirms UMC thereby grounds moral value in reason. An action has positive moral value in accord with the universal community of healthy interactions and negative value when it defeats its achievements. An action's positive moral value reflects the volume of moment it adds to the universal accord, and its negative moral value reflects the moment it exports from that accord.

In the sections ahead, I want to show how a basis for belief in UMC allows us to rethink the core claims of the standard meta-ethical positions—utility ethics, duty ethics, and virtue ethics. By transposing their key tenets and affirming them in new terms, they all become more intuitively true. On the other hand, if we try to adopt each as it is classically formulated, we blind ourselves to the others' intuitive insights. Accordingly, we will transpose the utility of happiness into the utility of moment, the categorical imperative into the personal imperative, and virtues into reliable ways to achieve optimal *momentum*. Doing that formulates a version of each that is immune to the standing lines of criticism leveled against it.

Utilitarian ethics

Utilitarians see moral value in terms of the consequences of an action, typically in terms of the happiness or unhappiness it occasions for everyone affected. If action A causes more happiness than action B, morally speaking A is the right thing to do. One of the attractions of this approach is that it makes room for something we intuitively know about actions, namely that they are morally good or bad *in measure*. Delaying one's errand for a few seconds to hold the door for someone has positive moral value, but not as much value as providing a home for a refugee family. This accommodation gives utilitarians a leg up on Kantian ethics and virtue ethics, both of which seem ill equipped to account for the *degrees* of blameworthiness or praiseworthiness we typically assign in making moral judgments. In that respect, utilitarian reasoning captures something true about moral value that eludes the others.

Our alternative way of thinking about the relative utility of a moral or immoral act is conducted in the language and logic of agency. There, the quantity of movement is implicit in the character of what we intend to do. It contributes to our sense of personal *momentum* in doing it. What we measure (in relative terms) is achievement, so presumably we assess the amount of an achievement by combining the moments of the moves in it. Having the capacity for imagining the achievement of everything we intend, our sense of what we intend is reasonable (or not). Like happiness utilitarians, *momentum* utilitarians measure goodness relatively, but we do it by deciding which option promises to actualize more moment. The two versions of utility have this in common: Both happiness and *momentum* are reasonable to assess comparatively without necessarily being explicitly quantified.

The advantage in transposing utility ethics from the logic of relative happiness to the logic of relative moment is that we escape the usual criticisms that the former are perennially challenged with. Here are a few examples:

1) Critics point out that if the *amount* of happiness an act occasions is what makes it good, the *source* of that happiness should not matter morally. Yet for most people it does matter. Even the most famous exponent of happiness utility, John Stuart Mill, thought that "[it] is better to be a human being dissatisfied than a pig satisfied; better to be Socrates dissatisfied than a fool satisfied. And if the fool, or the pig, are of a different opinion, it is because they only know their own side of the question."[3] That admission of common sense, however, posed a problem that did not go unnoticed. It failed to tell us how one could reasonably factor the quality of happiness with its amount to derive its value. Moreover, since we can only grasp relative happiness in our own life, we have no way to compare it with the happiness of other species. The same holds for the pig, which makes quality something of a conceptual loose end for Mill—something uncomfortably unscientific. He could assert the superiority of human happiness only by proceeding from the assumption that we, or at least those of us with Socratic sensibilities, discern qualities in our happiness that a pig cannot, and that if the pig shared our discernment, it would agree.

The need for Mill's dodge disappears when we construe what we are grasping as the combined momentary importance of various intention-satisfying actions. Pigs are agents with their own moments of intentional satisfaction, certainly. Yet the pig is not intending its action to accord with a complex intentional life the way we do. Our actions, like those of Socrates, intimate broader reaches of agency, so they are more momentous by virtue of their nuanced adverbial bearings. Since more courses of achievement mean more moment and more moment is good, the more momentous the act, the more positive utility it bears. It is for that reason that our lives carry more weight in moral deliberations than porcine ones.

2) Utilitarians are sometimes charged with failing to account for our sense of moral obligation. Critics point out the difference between figuring out which course promises to produce the most happiness and being motivated to take that course. Most of us, I suspect, pursue our own happiness more actively than that of others. David Hume and Adam Smith granted that tendency in us but accounted for it with a sympathy principle proposed to supplement that of utility.[4] They saw a sense of sympathy leading us to try to make others happy. Mill resisted adding sympathy to the moral calculus. Perhaps he reasoned that if he admitted a need for it, he would be admitting that happiness was not sufficient to account for moral value.

If Mill had been a moment utilitarian, he would not have needed to resist this solution. He would have seen in sympathy a mode of healthy interaction that generates moment as well. Creating moment in the life of another would have registered as positive utility on the same scale of intentional satisfaction as any other utilitarian consideration.

Recall Jill's sympathy for Jack's slightly damaged agency when she gave his jacket away. Her *sym-pathy*, *feeling-with*, Jack's hurt had a restorative function in that it led her to apologize and promise to amend her ways, thereby restoring their bonhomie. Acting sympathetically put her *with* Jack's struggle to recover lost agency; it made her a momentary partner.[5] The upshot is that sympathy can multiply one's agency as readily as any of the other modes of interaction we have looked at. Hume and Smith were right to insist that it is a crucial determinant of the moral value of interactions, but Mill was right to insist that reason is sufficient to the task.

3) Strict happiness utilitarians cannot admit that how an action *distributes* happiness is morally relevant. John Rawls was stirred to theorize about justice partly in response to the offense against fairness he saw in classical utilitarianism. It implies that even slavery would be moral if

the actual or anticipated pleasure it produced outweighed the enslaved people's unhappiness.[6]

Transposing reasoning about increments of happiness into reasoning about moments of active satisfaction dissolves the problem. A moral world precludes slavery because slavery constitutes a system of unhealthy relationships. If we believe in UMC, the prospect of a society where unhealthy relationships are institutionalized would be personally destructive for everyone involved.

4) Utilitarians insist that everyone's happiness should count equally in making moral decisions, but few of us act on that premise. Almost all of us feel a greater obligation to create happiness in ourself and our family and friends. Readers who sometimes follow discussions of ethical issues know that this split between intuition and reason has intrigued several generations of philosophers. Peter Singer's work, for example, found its way into most ethics course anthologies because it confronted this tension forthrightly. It urged us to surmount the popular proclivity—which most of us think is founded intuitively—much as we have surmounted other inherited irrational biases.

One current version of this approach, the effective altruism (EA) movement, provocatively stretches the scope of moral accountability by holding that the happiness of *all future generations* weighs equally with ours. To try to survey the scope of moral accountability implied here induces intellectual vertigo, and the unrelenting audacity of that approach has moved utility ethics back into the spotlight. What is compelling about the doctrine to morally minded people is that we all feel an obligation to future generations. Yet the staggering implications seem too much to process.

To take a critical stance on EA, consider how we might sort out what is right and wrong about it by measuring the moral value of an action in terms of the moments of *active* satisfaction it intends. By making the determination personal, we assess the *momentum* the intended achievement adds to our life. Since moral value must be personal to be authoritative, the increments of moral value must have utility in our greatest actualization as a character of resolve. In effect, that puts a limit to what we can assume responsibility for. We can only be obligated to achieve what we can imagine achieving. Our being as an agent anchors our accountability in the strata of whatever coordinated achievement we can imagine moving in. Consequently, the elasticity of our accountability is limited by the prowess of our imagination.

Notice why. If we think back over the imaginative steps taken in getting to moral accountability, we can see that our power to imagine what we intend diminishes as our accountability grows. When we resolve our actions in a purely self-regarding way, the path we project is wholly ours to determine and we can map it in some detail. But in personal relationships, where our intentions bear shared character, we determine the character of our interactive project collaboratively. Thus, the relational part of it cannot be as granulated in our imagination. In the further broadening of authorship represented by the legacy dimension of our intentional life, the character of the active satisfaction we resolve to make possible stretches the limits of what we can conceive. As we grow agentively into the lives of others and beyond into unknown people's future lives, what we project actualizing becomes more and more speculative. To the extent that it eludes characterization, it loses determinacy of value, and with it leverage in our deliberations. That is why charity appeals seed our imagination with pictures of people enjoying a life that our contribution promises to make possible.

Though the "longtermism" of EA, with its insistence that we create as much happiness as we can in an unforeseeable future, cuts itself off from the very source of personal obligation, it does have a certain moral insight that needs to be preserved. It challenges us to project our imagination further than we habitually do. The longer the span of time over which we can imagine creating active moment, the more moment we can resolve to generate and the more beneficent we can imagine being. Stretching our imagination leads us to consider giving to international agencies rather than to local ones even if we do have to rely on the testimony of others to imagine the good that we can do. On purely utilitarian grounds—be they units of happiness or moments of intentional satisfaction—that promises to project a course with greater moral value. But we must keep in mind that a moment-utility calculus is irreducibly personal, so we cannot be obligated to transcend the personal matrix for moral meaning.

5) To their further credit, utilitarian ethicists have prompted us to take animal welfare into account when we consider benefits and losses. After all, animals enjoy happy lives and suffer unhappy ones, so it would be arbitrary for us to consider our own happiness alone in assessing utility. This insight has sometimes prompted us to regulate factory farms, roadside zoos, and other places that wantonly expend animal happiness for the sake of humankind.

But the reasonableness of that concern for animals will be suspect unless we find a basis for valuing human happiness above animal happiness. Here, happiness utilitarians have a problem. Since happiness is classified as an experience, and since experiences, whether painful or pleasurable, obtain over a span of time, some utilitarians have been led to equate an hour of animal happiness with an hour of human happiness. This leads them to charge anyone who refuses to follow suit with being a "speciesist," someone who, like a sexist or racist, arbitrarily elevates the happiness of some agents over that of others.

We can see a fallacy operating here akin to the one that posed the Socratic versus pig happiness problem we discussed above. In this case, we would be led to blame a firefighter for saving the life of a child rather than a litter of puppies. Here, too, though, we avoid the problem by replacing "moments of happiness" with "moments of intended satisfaction." That way, instead of basing our kinship with animals on our common awareness of happiness and unhappiness, we base it on the relative volumes of moment involved in any agent's intended satisfactions. That diverts utilitarianism from a slippery slope leading to a denial of what is human about agency. We can respect animals as fellow agents with moments of intentional movement, yet also recognize the difference between the momentary being of human and non-human animals. The active life of a non-human animal has intrinsic value pegged on the same currency as ours. It bears momentary value, but its intended character bears far less of it than the moment intended in the active life of a human. Dogs and ducks mean what they do, but without a context of resolve, their actions lack the storied context that would give them much accordant significance. In the agentively relevant sense of the term, that makes them less important than we are.

Kantian ethics

The Kantian assessment of moral value finds goodness in a person's will insofar as it is guided by pure practical reason, and that, for Kant, requires reasoning with categories of action. Categorizing actions allows for formal validity, which presumably makes the reasoning "categorical" in the sense of unconditional as well as category based.

We saw in other contexts how reasoning with categories forces us to ignore an action's personal character, allowing us to grasp its meaning only in impersonal terms. This was hardly lost on Kant. He was aware that identifying someone's action as "stealing" or "promising without intending to keep the promise" abstracts from its personal context. But he thought it a cost we must bear to determine the relevant categorical imperative. He was willing to buy moral meaning at the expense of personal meaning.

Let me suggest that we can confirm Kant's insight that *reason* determines moral duty, provided we understand character logical reasoning as the relevant kind. In our kind of duty-based ethics, the personal imperative rather than the categorical one defines duty. That transposition allows us to avoid some of the standard criticisms leveled against Kantian ethics. By showing how shifting our reasoning fends them off, I mean to recommend it as a more satisfactory duty-based account of moral value.

1) Kant invites us to reason our way to an action's moral value starting with the category of action that impersonally describes its character, like "lying" or "stealing." Starting from the mere meaning of such terms, he proceeds to the conclusion that lying is wrong. (If everyone were permitted to lie, trust in communication would collapse and "lying" would lose its meaning. Or stealing is wrong because if everyone were free to steal, property rights would disappear and "stealing" would lose its meaning.) Some critics have pointed out, however, that we can imagine times when obeying the categorical imperative would lead one to commit a moral atrocity. As a rule, stealing is wrong . . . as a rule. But if Jack had a chance to foil a terrorist's bomb plot by stealing his detonator, he would do so without qualm. Generally, stealing is wrong because it represents a willfully unhealthy act. But not in this case. Why not?

Consider first what makes Jack's theft of the detonator personally imperative at the time. When he took it, his intention was to save lives. That intention had momentous legacy meaning in that disarming the terrorist made a great volume of active moment possible in others' lives, the lives of the people he was resolved to save. That makes it reasonable to conclude that in this instance, stealing is Jack's personal imperative.

But was it also his moral imperative? Common sense would say that it was. One would hope that anyone in Jack's position—able to spare unfathomable personal loss—would regard doing so as their moral duty. But (and this is the elephant in the room) this intuition seems at first glance to fly in the face of our contention that all moral interactions are healthy. Jack's theft appears to have constituted an unhealthy interaction with the terrorist. After all, he foiled his plans; he undid a big part of his intentional life. But that snap judgment fails to consider the matter under the UMC assumption. On that basis, the terrorist's act would be self-defeating, it being impossible for him to profit from exploiting others. By disabling the terrorist's resolve, Jack did the terrorist a favor, though the terrorist could only come to see this later, and then only if he developed a moral imagination. Persons are measured as characters of resolve by the volume of movement they intentionally achieve in acting as they do. The more intentional movement they actualize, the greater the person they are. People who are called great are called great for that reason. The same logic applies when the numbers are negative. It is possible for someone to be resolved to deactivate more life than they activate. In earlier times, we would call them demonic; now we would call them sociopathic. If UMC is true, the terrorist bears negative valence as an active being. He depletes more life out of the world than he adds. In stopping him, Jack prevents him from agentive oblivion and preserves the chance that he may yet be a "contributing" member of society. On that basis, Jack's interaction with him was healthy after all.

2) A related problem for Kant's duty ethics stems from the conflicting categorical imperatives people sometimes find themselves subject to. A security goon comes to the door of a good Kantian looking for the patriot he is harboring in his attic. "Is he here?" he asks. The Kantian recognizes his categorical obligation to tell the truth, yet he also feels categorically obligated to protect people from injustice. Lying is the only way to do the latter, but delivering his guest over to injustice is the only way to do the former. Damned if he tells the truth; damned if he doesn't. That puts him in a dilemma from which there is no Kantian escape, no *systematic* basis for determining which duty should take precedence. Suppose he takes what I trust we would agree is the moral path and lies to save the patriot. Later, presumably, he should feel good for having done something justifiable but also bad for having done something immoral. He would have to live with the odd fact that we are sometimes categorically obliged to do immoral things.

The conscience of the liar would be better served if he understood his duty as a personal imperative. Lying would then be justified by promising to actualize more intentional satisfaction than handing over the patriot did. The lied-to agent might suffer a bit of professional embarrassment for not locating the patriot, but that disappointment would weigh little against the life of active possibilities the harborer intends for the patriot fleeing injustice. Moreover, comparable to the case of Jack and the terrorist, we need not see his interactive lie as unhealthy. Arresting the patriot would have been a self-defeating act even though he does not have the moral imagination to realize it. The lie spared him great personal failure.

3) People typically attach an amount of praise or blame to their moral judgments. When we judge someone, we not only make a binary judgment (that the agent was morally justified or not) but also a relative one (about how praiseworthy or blameworthy they were). There is a wide spectrum of moral value from "that was a nice thing to say, Jill" to "saying that took real courage, Jill." The same goes for blameworthiness. Kant's binary—rational/irrational—cannot accommodate the relative judgments because they cannot factor in the relative moment being intentionally created or destroyed in that act. By defining the imperative as personal, we allow for that assessment.

4) Then there is the cold and bloodless way Kant's moral agents reason. As Philippa Foot points out, if Kant is right, neither love nor care can legitimately ground moral action.[7] For him, good-willed actors are category concerned but never context concerned. One consequence is that interpersonal affect never influences moral obligation. Another way to put this complaint is to say that Kant ignores the personal meaning of moral value. If we assume UMC, our personal imperative version of duty-based ethics becomes personal as well as moral: It determines the moral course as one of resolute action, which means it must be characterized personally, with all the emotions and affections thereunto appertaining. In a personalist version of duty-based ethics, there is no need to—and every reason not to—pretend that emotional meaning has no role determining moral value.

5) Finally, one of the most contested implications of Kant's ethics is its representation of punishment as retribution. From our standpoint, he was correct to identify offenders by the character of their offense but wrong to fix their personal identity by the nature of their wrongdoing. The cruel and counterintuitive implication of identifying someone that way, particularly when the offense was committed in the distant past, is that "justice" can only be served when the sentence is fully served. Strictly adhered to, that means practices like awarding time off for good behavior have to count as miscarriages of justice.

This harsh view has some supporters today, but I think it fair to say that most of us have deep misgivings about thinking of justice only as payback. Assuming we have developed sufficiently as an agent, we should have those misgivings. We meet people on a personal level in the character of their presence. When we interact with someone who has offended in the past, we hold open the possibility that their presence is no longer coherent with the character of criminal resolve they bore at the time of the offense. It makes sense for us to ask whether they are still present as a projected character in which criminal activity could still be resolved.

For our purposes, we can think of someone's criminal resolve simply as their resolve to exploit another in a way that breaks the criminal law. To justly convict such an offender, two things must be true. First, at the time of his crime, he was resolved to commit it, and second, his personal resolve now (at the time of the conviction) is coherent with his resolve when he offended. We assume, in other words, that he continues to be a character of criminal resolve. Of course, we could be mistaken about this, particularly if the offense was committed long ago and, unbeknown to us, the offender has since renounced and repudiated his former life of crime. It is not unheard-of for someone arrested for something they did thirty years ago to have lived for many years as an upright, contributing member of society. When we read about people like that, we are inclined to think that they should not be treated now in the same way they would have been treated thirty years ago.

This same possibility of re-narrativizing one's life applies to someone who has undergone years of confinement. It is relevant to ask whether they continue to be coherent with that chapter of their life or whether they have "reformed" in the sense that their present projection of life would be deactivated were they to take up criminal activity again. "Correction" has taken place if the *body* of intentional life they now project functions as an *antibody* to further criminal resolve. If such a "change of heart" has taken place and if it promises to be sustainable, society's interests have been satisfied and further detention would be cruel and pointless. For legal and moral purposes, the newly resolved person is no longer the person who offended. Criminal character has been deactivated; society's slate has been wiped clean.

In summary, Kant is right to insist that moral judgments are determined by reason alone, right to insist that we should respect the persons we judge, and right to identify persons according to the duties they obey and the permissions they grant themselves. But we can better preserve those insights about duty determining morality if we understand a person as an active character of resolve. It allows us to respect who they *are* and not trap them in a past they have repudiated.

Virtue Ethics

A compelling tradition that traces back to Aristotle bases moral value in the virtues associated with being human. He invited us to think of virtues as functional excellences that enable us to flourish. For much of that tradition, labels like honesty, courage, loyalty, and kindness identified them, but this of course raises a caution flag for us. We have seen how categorizing action can set traps for the understanding. To avoid being snared, we must designate the functional excellences as *personal* rather than *human*. By rethinking virtues in personal terms, they become manifestations of significance and importance in our personal life. That explains the volumetrics we use in describing how we feel when we are virtuous—how big-hearted, expansive, and proud—or wanting in virtue—petty, small, ashamed. In our version of virtue ethics, an act is virtuous if it creates the greatest moment, be it individually, interactively, as a legacy, or (most likely) as a compound of the three.

Self-discipline is typically a virtue one cultivates to flourish in perfecting their own projects. A concert pianist may modify a great deal of her life for the sake of her artistry and sacrifice much to cultivate it, but she is unlikely to see her life as one of self-abnegation. Quite the contrary, she sees long practice sessions as the way to advance the art that characterizes so much of her life and means so much to her.

The virtue of loyalty exemplifies functional excellence on the interactive level. Think of how friends adopt it to consolidate their relationship and instill deeper mutual trust. With loyalty comes a saturation of relational meaning and the expansion of each into their joint achievement.

The virtue of philanthropy fosters flourishing on the legacy level. It extends the donor's individual and interactive character beyond the immediacy of present interactions into a future of bequeathed *momentum*. Practicing charity is virtuous in that we create conditions for bringing lively possibilities into other people's futures, and even in future people.

There are, of course, a great many virtuous actions extending our agency on one, two, or all three vectors on which our resolve characterizes movement. For our purposes, we will concentrate on the interactive realm, since that is where the classic moral issues tend to arise. How then are we to transpose our traditional understanding of the interactive virtues, like honesty, compassion, fairness, and courage? By thinking of them as types of narratives instead of types of action. It is stories that characterize people as honest, as fair, and so forth. There is an analogy here with the narrative contexts that give emotions their meaning. Like them, virtues are usually referred to by using an exemplary narrative from a typology of them: Honesty is what George Washington practiced when asked if he chopped down the cherry tree, and steadfastness is what John McCain showed by enduring his captivity honorably. Yet we need to keep in mind that it is the force of the narrative action, not the type of narrative it is, that makes it virtuous for the actor.

With this transposition in mind, let us reconsider some of the complaints about virtue ethics from critics in the other camps.

1) We stipulated earlier that moral accountability is not limited to one's mores communities and that it must have "universal" accreditation such that an action would register as moral to any reasoning person of goodwill who was fully aware of its character in context. Does this requirement pose a particular challenge for virtue ethics?

Some think it does. Utilitarians, after all, can argue that any rational person could be expected to make the same judgment about the utility of an action if they were fully informed about its consequences. Presumably, if everyone acted realistically and abided by the greatest happiness principle, their actions would not conflict. Kantians can point to the purity of people's practical reasoning as guaranteeing the same outcome: If we all followed the categorical imperative, social and personal harmony would ensue across mores divides. Virtue ethicists have a less obvious claim on a universal standard for moral value. Different cultures confront us with different functional excellences. The military virtues of ancient Sparta, the chivalric ones in medieval Provence, and the civil ones of eighteenth-century Edinburgh are so distanced from one another by contingencies of place and time that it can be hard to imagine people in those cultures regarding the others' virtues as virtuous. For some, this relativity suggests that human virtues are fundamentally parochial.

The relativity objection misses its mark, however, if we assume universal moral community. It is true that the articulation of virtues is initially inculcated by the mores communities that nurtured us early on. But we have also seen that what such communities do cannot be said to have the final word on moral value, since they tend to call for "othering" non-members. But notice that cultural relativism can be a challenge to virtue ethics only if it turns out that acting in good faith requires people in one culture to counteract people in another. Since that is precisely what belief in UMC denies, a reasoned commitment to that belief supplies a defense against the charge. In fact, differently cultured communities interact all the time, and they usually get along fine. When they do not, chances are that othering is being used to promote mores solidarity. If we assume UMC, cross-cultural interactions can always be healthy to the betterment of all parties.

2) Virtue ethicists are sometimes challenged to define what it is that makes an action virtuous. Aristotle could meet this challenge with his teleological understanding of nature. He saw in every organism a mode of flourishing determined by its kind. Each mode constituted a virtue for that kind of agent. In our time, skepticism about natural types militates against justifying virtues that way, so Aristotle's determination of what counts as a virtue has largely lost its hold on our thinking. It is that loss that poses the challenge.

A promising way to meet it is to point to the broad agreement I think we have about what makes people flourish, one that sustains itself well enough even without belief in natural types. As Aristotle observed, we enjoy a sense of *well-being* when we truly flourish, a sense he called *eudaimonia*. We can think of it as our sense of inner accord when we act in good faith. If we take this sense of active accord as a mark of virtuous behavior—again, assuming UMC—virtue ethics has its cross-cultural criterion for personal virtuousness.

Not everybody will be satisfied with this appeal to a sense of well-being, to be sure. Some of their dissatisfaction, I suspect, stems from a limiting assumption fostered by modernity. As modern scientific thinking gained traction, it became common to bifurcate the determinants of action into subjective and objective factors. That intellectual strategy relegates feelings of well-being to the subjective realm, putting judgments about well-being beyond the reach of reason. Transposing the premises that construct the impasse restores a rational basis for our sense of well-being as well as affirms its status as a feeling. If I am right that Aristotle's sense of eudaimonia seems a good match with our sense of acting in good faith, and that actualizing ourself optimally justifies calling our action virtuous, confidence that we are acting in good faith and with goodwill is based in practical reasoning. Reason, then, can indeed function as a guide to abundant living.

3) Finally, in some critics' eyes, virtue ethics fails to provide an explicit formula for distinguishing right from wrong. Deontologists and utilitarians are largely focused on drawing that line persuasively, the former by determining the categorial imperative governing decisions, the

latter by weighing positive consequences against negative ones. Virtue ethicists disagree on that description of an ethicist's challenge. Instead of being concerned with distinguishing good actions from bad, they find it more rewarding to identify the practices that yield abundant and satisfying living. They look for them displayed in the narratives people tell of abundant and satisfying living.

The fact that there should be a philosophical dispute about the point of doing ethics is intriguing and disappointing, since most of us want it both ways. We want a formula to show us how our specific responsibilities are determined *and* we want a guide to leading a good life. Can we have it both ways? We can if we recognize action as virtuous for its moment-maximizing. That is the "formula." As for determining our life as good, if we enjoy a sense of well-being and feel well-grounded in our relational life and legacy, we have reason to feel virtuous.

I have been making the case that transposing the founding claims of the three dominant accounts of moral value formalizes a version of each that better squares with how we reason in practice and one that adequately answers its critics. Moreover, it is one that makes each compatible with the insights of the other two. Utilitarians are right to insist that our discernment of moral value is grounded in feeling—in their version, feeling happiness or pleasure; in ours, feeling *momentum*. Kantians are right to insist that pure practical reasoning determines the morality of an action—in their version, the categorical coherence of dutiful action; in ours, the narrative coherence of lives lived in adding to each other's agency. We can affirm virtue ethicists when they make personal flourishing the measure of what is right, and contribute an account of how that flourishing unfolds as internal integrity, relational health, and a wholesome legacy.

My argument leads to the conclusion that when ethical reasoning is underwritten by belief in UMC, it provides a rational account of moral value. If the reader shares the belief that we can, in good faith, find accord with all good-willed people, this chapter establishes moral value as an ingredient in the meaning of a person's action.

6

The Meaning of Life

The proverbial mountaintop guru, visited by an occasional truth seeker, always seems to get the same question: "What is the meaning of life?" In comic strips he often responds with a quip, "It's a subscription service and I'm still on a free trial" or "Look it up in the dictionary" or "42, obviously." If that kind of response is amusing, it is amusing for an interesting reason. Rather than answering the question, it dissolves it into laughter. Much like a Zen koan, it dispels question and questioner both.

But not everyone is willing to be put off with a joke. Some people persist in seeking an answer. They might even turn to a philosopher, thinking (or pretending to think) that if anyone can answer that question, they (we) can. I mean to take them up on the challenge. First, though, we must agree on what the question means. Our medieval predecessors saw themselves as microcosms ensconced in a macrocosm, all of it a composite of earth, water, air, and fire. They lived out their lives in a geography between heaven and hell, and what they did in life had meaning and purpose in the drama being played out in that whole/holy scheme.

In modernity, after emergent cosmologies replaced old ones, the new ones no longer purported to contextualize life's meaning. Quite to the contrary, they challenged people's confidence that life had meaning "in the greater scheme of things." By the nineteenth century, writers like Kierkegaard, Nietzsche, and Dostoyevsky spoke to the breakdown of the old consensus and thematized the anxiety its dissolution fed. Paul Tillich called it an "anxiety of meaninglessness," "anxiety about the loss of an ultimate concern, of a meaning which gives meaning to all meanings."[1] In light of this crisis of meaning, the guru trope becomes wistful as well

135

as whimsical. We testify to its appeal by continuing to ask the question of life's meaning even when we doubt the possibility of a serious answer.

In this chapter, I want to back into an answer to that question by describing some of the ways we are aware of the absence of life's meaning. We will observe some of the features of anxiety in the face of the loss of life's meaning, particularly those that are determined by the correlation we have been exploring between a loss of active meaning and a loss of intended movement. In chapter 4 we described how our sense of diminished movement registers as negative emotion. That understanding suggests we might learn something about anxiety by treating it as a negative emotion and describing our awareness of it as that of slowed *momentum*. Reasoning from that three-way correlation, it appears that at last part of the loss of meaning is attributable to losing our status as movement in a universal drama. When the scientific era disconnected us from any encompassing scheme of meaning/movement/moment, we became disenchanted. We found the impersonal cosmological context for our life unsupportive of anything we would call "ultimate" meaning. We saw the impersonality of the world precluding it from functioning as a dimension of personal meaning.

At the root of such disconsolation is a misplaced disappointment, one grounded in an assumption that, if there is ultimate personal meaning, it must be contextualized in the language and logic of impersonal cosmology. Impersonal meaning cannot contain personal meaning any more than personal meaning can contain impersonal meaning. The only way to play the guru is to explore the meaning of life as the meaning of personal life and to ask about an "ultimate" meaning for life in personal terms.

Ordinarily, at this stage of the exposition I would try to sharpen my account by playing it off against some others offered by other writers who have discussed the topic. On this question, however, most philosophers have left the debate stage. Those on the continent are mostly off celebrating the contingency of meaning, which they think precludes making sense of the question. They think that whatever steers the events of meaning-giving—be it power differentials among genders, races, or classes, or more loosely a generalized aleatory tumble—it precludes *the* meaning of anything, much less *the* meaning of a person's life. Anglo-American philosophers have not paid much professional attention to the guru question either. But neither have they ignored it systematically. Happily, for our purposes their efforts provide enough grist for one last mill run.

One issue dividing philosophers who discuss the "meaning of life" has to do with its source. It seems generally agreed on that we should think of that source as either subjective or objective. The line gets variously drawn, but everyone seems to agree that it is a line that must be drawn. Widely agreed on as well is the assumption that an internal/external distinction maps onto the subjective/objective one. Subjectivists hold that processes internal to us underwrite whatever meaning our life has; objectivists hold that the values that give life meaning must be founded on something external to our feelings. Among objectivists, some hold out for standards of meaningfulness that all rational people could accept, while others more modestly find sufficient objectivity in the views shared in their communities.

My millstone will rotate in the usual direction, surveying some examples of accounts from both subjectivist and objectivist camps, then noting some seemingly intractable problems challenging each, then transposing their language into the language and logic of agency, and finally recommending the transposition as avoiding those seemingly intractable problems.

Subjectivist Accounts

Subjectivists point to factors within us—like capacities, commitments, and feelings—as sources of the meaning we find in life. In the *Stanford Encyclopedia of Philosophy*, Thaddeus Metz surveys such accounts, and I use the types he discusses to organize our observations.

> Some contend that feelings are key, so that life's meaning consists in being satisfied with one's choices or absorbed by one's activities. Others hold that life's meaning is a function of inclinations, for example, desiring something and getting it or obtaining what one would favor from a certain standpoint. Still others believe that choices are essential to life's meaning, namely, adopting purposes and acting to realize them. Finally, there are those who maintain that meaningful aspects of a life turn on beliefs, say, achieving what one judges to be important. As this last example indicates, combinations of these elements are to be expected. One carefully articulated view that combines several subjective conditions is that of Harry Frankfurt, who maintains that one's life is significant if one loves something.[2]

Metz starts by discussing the position that *feelings* are the source of life's meaning. A. J. Ayer, for one, specified feelings of satisfaction with the activities we are absorbed in as that source. Some have countered that this would allow for someone to count as having a meaningful life even if his deep satisfaction came with making handwritten copies of *War and Peace*, solving Sudoku puzzles, or tending to a pet goldfish (Susan Wolf's vivid examples). Seemingly, Ayer cannot accommodate our intuitive sense that only some of the things people get absorbed in count as satisfying in a way that makes life meaningful.

While Ayer's account does seem insufficient in that respect, he seems right to insist that having feelings of satisfaction is part of finding life meaningful. It would be odd to say that someone who is unsatisfied with what she was doing with her life was nonetheless leading a life full of meaning. But notice how we accommodate Ayer's point by locating the basis for endorsing satisfactions and absorptions in our active awareness rather than in our felt sensibilities. To be actively aware of being *satisfied* is to be aware of having *made-enough* movement to achieve what we intend. Similarly, activities that *ab-sorb* us, that *suck* us *in*, are those that most characterize us personally. Ayer is right to recognize satisfaction and absorption as crucial to a meaningful life, but wrong to trace life's meaning to raw feelings, which have no intrinsic meaning. What we are greatly satisfied in doing and what we are most absorbed in doing are activities we are personally resolved in doing. That is what makes them the source of life's meaning.

Another subjectivist proposal defines a meaningful life as one that fulfills one's *desires*. This might sound plausible, at least initially. After all, if our desires were being frustrated at every turn, that would seem to diminish our life's meaning. But there is a problem with designating desire-satisfaction as the mark of a meaningful life, one akin to the quality of satisfactions problem. Unless we have a basis for separating meaning-generating desire from trivial or harmful desire, we have to say that an especially avid internet troll leads just as meaningful a life as someone with good work and good friends. But, again, if we shift from using desire-fulfilling language to using intention-satisfying language, we register our intentions as variously meaningful according to the moments of movement they intend. The most meaningful of them are the most momentous, and their relative scope can be discerned by our active imagination.

If none of these subjectivist theories by itself successfully accounts for the way we judge that some lives are more meaningful than others, might not an account that combined their features do the trick? Merz cites Harry Frankfurt's work on the topic as aiming to do just that. Frankfurt holds that our *love* for something makes our life meaningful. He knows that some people may object to that claim by arguing that love can be just as undiscerning of relative meaningfulness as the other subjective traits. But he has a rebuttal to that objection. Love enhances the lover's freedom in a unique way. Our loving puts "an end to indecisiveness concerning what to care about."[3] It takes away indifference and settles ambivalences that would otherwise "impair our capacity to choose and to act." For Frankfurt, loving is liberating in much the same way that our escape from adolescence was liberating: by coordinating us as intentional agents so that one part of our intentional life does not disappoint another. Loving another, Frankfurt says, makes "it impossible for us to exercise, for the sake of other goals that we happen to find appealing, control over the formation of our beliefs and our will." Frankfurt's love stabilizes life by ending at least some of the paralyzing indecisiveness suffered because of competing intentions.

Certainly, there is something to this. Sometimes people say things like, "Falling in love was good for him because it settled him down." It seems reasonable to say that a great many people benefit from loving relationships in just that way. But as an account of love securing meaning in life, it seems descriptively thin. As we saw in chapter 2, the distinctive mode of togetherness friends and lovers enjoy transcends their individual boundaries. That means their agency grows, a claim that subjectivists, who locate a person's subjectivity internal to one body, cannot account for. They cannot appreciate how lovers' sense of shared *momentum* puts them in the same interactive moment and how it enhances the movement of each. By coordinating their respective characters of resolve, the two beloveds mutually enrich the meaning of both their lives.

Objectivist Accounts

Objectivists site the source of life's meaning outside of and apart from how we feel about our life. One way they challenge subjectivist accounts is to recall the ancient Greek story of Sisyphus, the defier of the gods, who was condemned to carry a rock up a hill, then let it roll down again, repeatedly, eternally. We shudder to contemplate his life because it seems like a perfect emblem for meaninglessness. If we asked a subjectivist why

Sisyphus's life was meaningless, presumably their only recourse would be to blame Sisyphus's emotional state. He needs an attitude adjustment. If he were more like Disney's seven dwarfs, singing in the new day with "Hi-Ho, Hi-Ho, it's off to work we go!," he would see life as meaningful.

First, notice why Sisyphus's life strikes us as meaningless. If we think of him as a person, he presents as an emblem of futility because the gods have denied him personal meaning on all three vectors of meaningful vitality. He is mono-intentional, so what he is doing resolves nothing. He is solitary, so his action has no interactive or relational meaning. And, since the stone rolls back down every time, what he does can bear no intended legacy. On every count, his action is deprived of personal meaning.

If this is a plausible description of why Sisyphus leads a meaningless life, we might ask whether it qualifies as an objective account. It counts as objective in our terms in that it universalizes the criterion for a relatively meaningful life. Its measure—that of momentary satisfaction on the three vectors of agency—applies to all agents regardless of species or culture. This version of objectivity gives us an advantage over other objectivists, which we can see by looking at a few of their versions and then noting how ours answers the challenges theirs are subject to. Here, too, I use Thaddeus Metz's essay as our guide to their positions and vulnerabilities.

Metz finds all of them deficient in that they fail to provide a general, unified account of what makes projects objectively attractive as sources of meaning.[4] For instance, he cites Richard Taylor's theory that "a life is meaningful just insofar as it is creative."[5] But, as Metz points out, this leaves out any moral dimension of a meaningful life, and compassion and kindness, among other habits of the heart, are widely taken to be ingredients in meaningful living.[6] But if we rethink creativity by representing it as novel actualization, Taylor's creativity can have intrinsic moral meaning: The story we project on the wings of our narrative imagination creates moments of satisfaction—moments of making enough movement toward what we intend—not only in our life but in the lives of our interactors and deferred beneficiaries as well. Admittedly, that only amounts to a defense against the charge of amorality if we can justify belief in UMC. But if we do assume that a life of goodwill can always be lived in good faith—the assumption that it can be lived in UMC—then the moral value of a creative life is objective.

Robert Nozick proposes that the objective source for life's meaning is self-transcendence and connection to what is beyond ourself. That connection, he thinks, is organic, and he offers the activity of painting as an example. The painter integrates colors, forms, and symbols, and in so doing externalizes himself by connecting with those who appreciate his art. Likewise with acts of kindness in which we transcend into the well-being of another.[7]

Nozick's account has a great deal of resonance with our notion of the imaginative feats wherein our actions take on relational character as well as individual meaning. For example, it is easy for us to hear Nozick's point about "being organically connected with what transcends us" as a variation of "being coordinated with others in a common achievement." Imagine Nozick's painter's painting being exhibited. We can then imagine a viewer's imagination being informed by the "work," the work of integrating colors, et cetera. His work, in effect, is extending into her life as she tries to take a complementary imaginative leap to integrate those elements for herself. Likewise with acts of kindness that open active possibilities in others, possibilities they otherwise wouldn't have. By creating greater moment in the lives of others, we transcend our individuality.

The advantage of making the point about self-transcendence in terms of interactive and legacy living is that it then becomes intrinsic to our identity. There is no natural limit to the achievement defining our personhood. But as Metz points out, Nozick's assumptions about human agency seem to impose limits. What can it mean "to 'transcend limits,'" he asks, "when the item beyond the limits is a state internal to the person?"[8] That criticism does not apply to Nozick's point under a character-of-resolve reading of persons. No longer need we recognize an implicit immanent/transcendent boundary applicable to personal agency.

Finally, Metz considers Alan Gewirth's proposal that we think of a meaningful life as one that "exceptionally employs reason." For Gewirth, this means "going beyond one's animal self to a greater degree than people typically do," be it in creating works of art or doing the right thing in the face of temptation.[9] Metz thinks Gewirth's account is the most promising of the objectivist views, though not without its own shortcomings. It fails to "account for the way that the overall pattern of a life could help to constitute its meaning. Many people believe that a life with unity or progression is more meaningful than one with fragmentation or repetitiveness."[10] In Metz's eyes, Gewirth's "reason" cannot account for the unity and progression he finds ingredient in life's meaning. But again, if we transpose Gewirth's contention that a meaningful life is one that "exceptionally employs reason" so that it reads "exceptionally employs personal practical reason," then a person's reasoning generates both narrative integrity and agentive reach. In that sense, it provides the unity and progress Metz is looking for.

Hybrid Accounts of Meaningfulness

To some philosophers, it seems clear that a reasonable account of life's meaning should recognize both our feelings about what we do and some measure of the relative value of those activities, one that is calculated on a basis that is in some sense objective. Two such accounts have recently been advanced: Todd May's *A Significant Life* and Susan Wolf's *Meaning in Life and Why It Matters*. Each tests a version of "objectivity" for its adequacy in underwriting relative meaningfulness.

May finds our life's significance in the "narrative values" we live out:

> Our lives gain meaningfulness when we are engaged in a life trajectory that expresses one or more narrative values. When we are absorbed in the unfolding of our life, when it makes sense to continue to do what we do, when we endorse our projects: that is half of it. When that unfolding occurs by subtlety or integrity or intellectual curiosity or intensity or any other positive value that would capture its temporal character, then we have the other half of it. To the extent that these two halves meet, we have a meaningful life.[11]

The first half, the subjective factors, is complemented by a second set based on how subtle, and/or how integral, and/or how curious, and/or how intense, and so forth, our activities are. Some combination of these narrative values underwrites our sense of meaningfulness in life. To understand how narrative value is perceived, May invites us to make sense of people's lives not in terms of their individual acts but in terms of their practices or ways of doing things. As we conduct our life, our actions defer to one another and criticize one another in a holistic network of know-how. That network is the "object" in objective. Its values are confirmed in practice by one another, not "written into the nature of things"[12] nor justified "from the standpoint of the universe."[13] What grounds and justifies their narrative value is that same "web of values and practices that constitute a community's life."[14] May finds "objectivity" of this sort sufficient to his purpose, which is to establish narrative value as non-arbitrary. He insists that any further grounding is not only unnecessary but also amounts to what Camus called "philosophical suicide," a refusal to accept the universe's ultimate absurdity.

In May's samples of narrative values—courage, intellectual curiosity, intensity, spirituality, and steadfastness—one hears an echo of Aristotle's "virtues." May resists that word, since Aristotle thought of virtues as having value relative to a *telos* grounded in nature. Since we are post-Aristotelian in that respect, May feels compelled to forego the conceit that there is a "foundation of values that everyone must agree on."[15] The values of our communal practices give us what sense we have of acting meaningfully.

May's regard for narrative values as being founded in shared practices squares nicely with our discoveries about interactive meaning and the *momentum* it adds to our life. Yet he cannot find any basis for universal agreement across communities of shared practices. Though May's objectivity may guarantee non-arbitrariness, it stops short of pointing to a universally accepted measure of narrative value. In that sense, life's meaning is not "ultimate." But, as we saw in our discussion of virtue ethics, there is no need to foreswear a basis for universal agreement. We can affirm it without committing "philosophical suicide" by affirming, as the universally applicable measure of value, the moments of intentional satisfaction we actualize in our practices. It is either objectively true or false that the narratives we live in actualize the greatest accord in our lives, health in our relationships, and a positive impact on posterity.

Susan Wolf's *Meaning in Life* draws on another kind of objectivity, one that finds affinity with Aristotle's "endoxic method." The *endoxa* (quoting Aristotle's *Topics*) are "the things which are accepted by everyone, or by most people or by the wise."[16] In other words, "common sense." Of course, some of what people think of as common sense is foolishness, so it would be foolish to anchor the objective pole of life's meaning in common "common sense." Rather, the standard should be the common sense of wise people. Wolf sees no way to universalize the reasoning that establishes that wisdom. She does not think we can lay it out explicitly so that every rational person could recognize it as rational, but Wolf thinks we can depend on endoxic thinking to support the recognition of what she calls an "objective attractiveness" in some of the objects to which we are subjectively attracted.

Wolf's recipe for meaningful lives—blend "subjective attraction" with "objective attractiveness"—captures the combination we look for in an account of life's meaning. It explains why we would find so little meaning in a life of tending a goldfish. From our perspective, though, Wolf is settling for less than we need to. We do not have to accept less than full-throated objectivity in the reasoning of our endoxic method, not if we chart our inferences using character logic. We perceive meaning/movement/moment objectively, and our assessment of its value would be shared by any rational person who could fully understand the personal meaning of what we are doing.

We have been looking at some of the ways imposing a subjective/objective dichotomy in discussions of life's meaning creates false issues. Our account of personal meaning supersedes them by recognizing both our awareness of life's meaning as self-awareness, hence "subjectively grounded," and our reason-based ability to assess its relative moment, hence "objectively grounded."

The Meaning of Life as Momentary

To close out this account of how to think about life's meaning, I want to highlight how the temporal logic of personal meaning bears on our discussion. The premise to keep in mind is that personal meaning has its matrix in the meaning of someone's present moment of resolve. In the active sense of the term, personal meaning is "momentary." That does not make it a snapshot on the chronological continuum. It is saved from ephemerality by having its character necessarily contextualized in a story that projects past, present, and future actions . . . a personal story. Embedded in narrative temporality, an active moment's meaning can be replete with the full import of a life's historical meaning.

It is the function of this storied context to maintain optimal present resolve, and its success determines the reasonableness of our appraisal of life's meaning. By seeing that the character of present resolve trails its past and projects its future, we can see why a life's meaning can vary from richly momentous to agentively impoverished, depending on what "we're going through" at the time. Those same vectors and variations of active meaning explain why we see some people leading more meaningful lives than others.

One thing our account cannot do is provide a script for the guru. Recognizing life's meaning as momentary and its significance contextualized in an implicit narrative makes it impossible to proclaim from the mountaintop what life's meaning is. It is inexplicable because the context enriching it, monitoring it, guiding it, and enveloping it is tacit rather than explicit. We know its presence only as the accordant meaning of whatever we are attending to, so we cannot claim to know it objectively or give it figure. In fact, we recognize attempts to do so as idolatry.

Since this epistemic elusiveness makes it impossible to direct our attention to it, here too we must resort to backing into the issue by describing episodes of active awareness in which life becomes drained of personal meaning. An awareness of that absence might silhouette the formal shape of its presence. We will start with the most benign loss of meaning, simple boredom, then go on to illustrate a case where the meaning-drain threatens the coherence that individualizes us as persons, and end with a fanciful case where the loss of meaning/movement/moment is so severe that personal being is unsustainable.

It may be helpful to pause just long enough to notice how our proposal to discuss boredom as a deficit in active meaning represents a departure from the standard depiction of boredom, which makes it a condition of being inadequately stimulated. Making boredom the absence of experience may seem to make it more quantifiable than a loss of *momentum*, but I believe that it fails to describe adequately what boredom means to us personally. If we were to ask a bored person why she was bored, I doubt that she would complain about a lack of stimulation. More likely, she would complain that "there's nothing to do."

Boredom in the deactivating sense of having "nothing to do" can come about under a variety of conditions that differ in personal significance. First, the least threatening. All of us get bored sometimes. We find ourself "stuck" someplace, stuck in in the sense of not being able to move any part of our agenda: at a bus stop without a book or phone, or at home alone in the evening when the power fails. To describe such times in terms of the levels of our active awareness—attentive, adverbial, and accordant—we are temporarily attentively unoccupied. No intention on our agenda invites our attention. Except in extraordinary cases, being stuck this way is temporary—the bus arrives, the power flickers back on—and when it does, we quickly get back to paying attention to something needing or exciting our attention.

On an up-down scale, being bored counts as "downtime"; nobody feels "up" when they are bored. That fact points to a loss of boring moments' meaning. If we try to reason about all this in terms of experiential deprivation, we fail to appreciate the personal threat posed by even such passing periods. Albeit very temporarily, we become aware of shrinkage in our agency. In the panoply of our undertakings, of course, life goes on, since most of our present projects are still being advanced as intended. Overall *momentum* is only marginally affected. It amounts only to a brief letup of movement in one minor precinct of our agency. But during the time we attend to nothing, there can be no accordant meaning as a context for the meaning of what we are attentively doing. That makes these moments of boredom cold reminders that persons are agents. We live or die by doing or not doing. With our temporary loss of much of our active awareness, the moment becomes a memento mori, an intimation of life's momentary nature.

A more serious "nothing to do" situation would be one that did not just intimate a threat but posed one. If someone were prevented from moving any meaningful elements of their intentional life for an extended period of time, boredom could go from a sense of the fragility of personal agency to facing a genuine threat to its continuance. A prolonged inability to advance one's personal story would threaten its dissolution and with it the very possibility of personal meaning. An example of this level of threat can be found in Charles Dickens's novel *Tale of Two Cities*. The unrelenting boredom suffered by Dr. Alexandre Manette during his eighteen-year imprisonment in the Bastille left him so depersonalized at the time of his release that his family and friends wondered if he could recover his identity. Before confinement, he had been a renowned physician, but deprived of his practice or almost any other useful activity, he came close to a "breakdown." Ceasing to have a complex agenda as his projects fell away, he almost disintegrated. Happily, he was not irretrievably lost. By focusing relentlessly on shoemaking, a trade he took up in prison, he was able to hold onto a thread of sanity and escape personal oblivion.

There is one more level of deactivation in the state of having "nothing to do." It is represented by another fictional figure who is not given a personal name by his author because this figure does not represent a continuing character of resolve. Søren Kierkegaard's "Diary of a Seducer"[17] introduces us to someone called "A" who has no personal story in the sense of projecting a course that bears continuities as well as discontinuities with earlier episodes. Without one, he suffers a void of personal meaning in his life. The seducer reveals in his diary how he intentionally manipulated a young woman into falling in love with him and then manipulated her into turning her love into hate. Everything he did was coordinated to advance that plan. When the affair ended, meaningful agency itself went into abeyance until another temporary project took its place. His life was merely a succession of such projects. In the interims, when there was no focus for his life, Kierkegaard sees him as despairing at having no personal being. With no coherence to give his actual presence contextual meaning, he is unable to be a person. He is doomed to be capable only of impersonal action.

These three modes of having "nothing to do" are modes of boredom in that generic sense, and all of them illustrate ways life's meaning can be threatened. We can formally describe them as modes of active awareness bereft of adverbial and accordant meaning, moments of life without personal meaning.

We have had to admit that we cannot provide the guru with a summary answer to the question he keeps being asked. But now let us suppose that the guru sees life's meaning as personal. Suppose she is, in that sense, a personalist guru. Then the only way she can be helpful will involve finding out something about the seeker's life as he projected it. Given that she expects the meaning of his life to be correlated with the scope of his intended achievements, she would listen for how he imagined that scope. Her understanding of personal agency and accountability leads her to expect people to project with one of two assumptions operating. They believe either that there is or is not UMC drawing the lives of good-willed people into universal resolution.

Those seekers who find no reason to believe in UMC—we will call them the secular seekers—frame that scope differently than those who do believe. Secular seekers seek relative meaning. The most they can hope for is a life that projects most of its intentions in accord, that interacts in mostly healthy ways, and whose impact on others is more important than exportant. Their aspirations to having a meaningful life are this-worldly. Personal meaning for them is contained in the brief and fragile life they lead, plus in the hope of a legacy, if only for a generation or two, in others' fond memories.

The believers in UMC seek not only this-worldly meaning for their life, though they certainly want that. They seek assurance that their life can have ultimate meaning. What they mean by "ultimate" is inchoate conceptually, but its meaning is informed by the ultimacy represented by UMC. Meaning on an individual level is ultimate if it enjoys perfect internal accord, relational meaning is ultimate if it is unfailingly healthy, and legacy meaning is ultimate if it advances the coordinated body of—which is to say the personal life of—a universal moral community. We saw in the last chapter that UMC as an actual community would have the form of a person, a Person, a Character of ongoing Resolve, specifically the Character of the resolution of all people of goodwill. That is why God is the name of ultimacy in character logic and why belief in God gives ultimacy to the meaning of life when we reason with the logic of personal agency.

Suppose that the ultimate meaning seeker approaches the guru and is told that UMC is ultimate meaning. Suppose he then asks for confirmation that UMC is actual. But what the seeker now asks can only be answered by the seeker's own awareness. Is he aware of acting with integrity as an individual and in a healthy interactive life, and does he flourish in the confidence that he can find common cause with all good-willed people?

If he does, but only if he does, his life has ultimate personal meaning.

Glossary

The account developed in this book introduces no new vocabulary, but it does use ordinary words as terms of art. Nonetheless, they do largely reflect the *ordinary* uses we make of them. Because *systematic* uses of some of them have shifted, they have become detached from their etymons. These shifts can make it a challenge to hear them in their original, pre-modern sense, the sense we recall and use in this account. This glossary anticipates instances when the divergence may be confusing. The entries are roughly in the order in which they are introduced in the book.

Active awareness: our awareness of doing something. I may be aware of brushing my teeth, chatting with a friend, asking something of AI, or planning a trip. Active awareness typically has three layers of meaning, an **attentive meaning**, the meaning of the accomplishment we are paying attention to ("I'm driving to the airport"); an **adverbial meaning**, the adverbial modifications we make in how we do what we are doing so as to accommodate it to other things we are doing ("I'm driving fast to catch a plane"); and an **accordant meaning**, our sense of how this action fits into the rest of our life ("That flight is the only possible connection to my flight to Europe").

Intention: the way we stretch into an achievement by moving through time and space. Intended movement has the character of a trajectory of movement. Being aware of one's intention as a course of action is a necessary condition for coordinating the movements needed to achieve it.

Resolve: our coordination of the achievement of several intentions. We resolve to do something by modifying the way we intend to achieve various elements of our life. When we are highly resolved to do something, we modify a great deal of our intentional life to facilitate its accomplishment.

Character of action: what we mean to be doing, what we intend to achieve. It is what the coordinated succession of moves we are making signifies as a totality.

Character of resolve: what we intend to do when our movement aims to satisfy more than one item on our agenda. It represents a coherent course going forward meant to achieve several elements of our intentional life. Typically, we characterize resolve narratively.

Character of a person: the sense of the normative coherence of what we are doing with our intentional life as a whole. It represents the overall resolution of our intentional life, and its figure in our awareness is that of a protagonist in a personal story.

Agent: any being we identify by its action.

Multi-intentioned agents: those agents who can and do advance multiple intended projects simultaneously. This kind of agency is distinctively human.

Moment of action: the duration of the movement it takes to achieve that action.

Moment of resolve: the moment in which we project our course to satisfy multiple intentions. Moments of resolve generally have a greater temporal scope than unresolved actions, since they simultaneously advance multiple intentions. Because of their broader scope, we commonly think of them as being "of greater moment" or "more momentous."

Personal resolve: the overall coordination of our personal life we are trying to sustain in moments of resolve.

Personal identity. the character of personal resolve projected as the best way to coordinate our life at the time, including how we conduct our interactions and what legacy of active possibilities we create in the lives of other people. These are all ways that we create movement in the character of our resolve. That makes them elements of our identity as an individual agent.

Personal story: a narrative-like imaginative projection of our life into a future in which we accommodate the elements of our present intentional life as well as we can. Having a personal story requires projecting present resolve as the continuance of a personal past, one disclosed in certain past moments of resolve, specifically those that are narratively coherent with our present project. Our story includes the ways of resolving past actions that continue to inform the task of coordinating our life now. Thus, unlike a conventional story, a personal story relates past, present, and future actions.

Personal meaning: the meaning of what we are doing contextualized by our personal story.

Personal imperative: the imperative to actualize ourself most fully as a person. To do so, we must resolve our life as much as possible, since only by doing so can we achieve all we intend to accomplish.

Interaction: the movements of two or more people coordinated to achieve some shared intention.

Healthy interaction: one in which the parties intend their mutual success as agents; neither intends to interact to the other's disadvantage.

Unhealthy interaction: one in which one party tries to deactivate the other for their own agentive advantage.

Good faith: the confidence that our present action is advancing the course that promises to achieve more of what we intend than any other.

Goodwill: the intent to have only healthy interactions with others, or alternatively not to interact with them.

Deliberation: consideration of various courses of action to assess the moments of intention-satisfying movement they represent. On that basis, we judge which course promises to import the most movement into our intentional life. It thus registers as the most important thing to do.

Personal *momentum*: the global sense of moving on courses needed to achieve what we intend. It represents a temporal volume of movement, which is to say a body of intended achievement. It is the voluminous body of action we are is presently advancing on multiple fronts.

Positive emotion: an immediate awareness of accelerating *momentum*.

Negative emotion: an immediate awareness of decelerating *momentum*.

Universal moral community (UMC): a belief that it is always possible to act in good faith without having to exploit others and that it is always possible to find resolution with the projects of others of goodwill.

Notes

Introduction

1. Because the term "self-actualization" has been popularized by Abraham Maslow, I should note how my usage differs from his. For Maslow, self-actualization is the pinnacle atop the pyramid of human needs. From the bottom of the pyramid to its top, we strive to meet, in turn, biological and physical, security and safety, belongingness and love, self-esteem and awareness, aesthetics, and cognitive needs to be self-actualized. Each level of need builds on the other, but all are present throughout one's life. How thoroughly they can be met at any given point is relative. For example, it is hard to learn to appreciate philosophy or enjoy a Barber adagio (cognitive or aesthetic) if you are starving (biological/physical). I believe my use of the term is compatible with Maslow's, but I use it only to designate the mere fact of actualizing what we intend.

2. G. E. M Anscombe, *Intention*, 2nd ed. (Harvard University Press, 1963), 40.

Chapter 1

1. Donald Davidson, *Essays on Actions and Events* (Oxford University Press, 1980), 4.

2. A. I. Melden, *Free Action* (Routledge and Kegan Paul, 1961), 19.

3. R. Swinburne, *The Evolution of the Soul* (Clarendon Press, 1986), 87.

4. R. M. Hare, *The Language of Morals* (Clarendon Press, 1952), 20.

5. Sarah Stroud and Larisa Svirsky, "Weakness of Will," in *Stanford Encyclopedia of Philosophy* (Stanford University, 1997–), published May 14, 2008; last modified September 4, 2019; https://plato.stanford.edu/archives/win2021/entries/weakness-will/.

6. Rene Descartes, *Meditations on First Philosophy*; repr. in "Dreams and Dreaming," in *Stanford Encyclopedia of Philosophy* (Stanford University, 1997–),

published April 9, 2015, last modified November 27, 2019, https://plato.stanford.edu/entries/dreams-dreaming/.

7. Sharon M. O'Brien, "The Importance of Dreams," *Clinical Advisor*, December 15, 2016, https://www.clinicaladvisor.com/home/the-waiting-room/the-importance-of-dreams/.

Chapter 2

1. A. J. Ayer, *The Meaning of Life* (Charles Scribner's Sons, 1990), 193.

2. René Girard gave a name to this overlap in agency. He called it "interdividuality." In the people he studied as an "ethologist"—one who explores the continuities in social forms between animals and humans—he found a sense of being incorporated in bodies of cooperative accomplishment. *Things Hidden since the Foundation of the World*, trans. Stephen Bann and Michael Metteer (Stanford University Press, 1978), 35.

3. This way of drawing the distinction was standardized in Brown and Gilman, "The Pronouns of Power and Solidarity," in *Style in Language*, ed. T. A. Sebeok (MIT Press, 1960), 253–76.

4. Deevers, "End 'No Fault Divorce,'" *American Reformer*, December 2, 2023, https://americanreformer.org/2023/12/end-no-fault-divorce/.

5. These are the areas of agreement discussed by Bennett Helm in his entry on friendship in the *Stanford Encyclopedia of Philosophy* (Stanford University, 1997–), published May 17, 2005; last modified July 30, 2021, https://plato.stanford.edu/entries/friendship/.

6. *Physics*, 202b5.

7. See Elijah Milgram, "Aristotle on Making Other Selves," *Canadian Journal of Philosophy* 17, no. 2 (1987): 368.

8. Aristotle, *Nicomachean Ethics* 1166a, *The Basic Works of Aristotle*, edited and intro. Richard McKeon (Random House, 1941).

9. Michel de Montaigne, *Selected Essays with La Boetie's Discourse on Voluntary Servitude*, trans. James B. Atkinson and David Sices, intro. and notes James B. Atkinson (Hackett, 2012), 80.

10. Ibid., 73, note.

11. Ibid., 79.

12. Ibid, 81.

13. Bennett Helm, "Friendship."

14. Joseph Wood Krutch, *Samuel Johnson* (Henry Holt & Company, 1944), 107.

15. American Academy of Pediatrics, "Clinical Report—The Impact of Social Media on Children, Adolescents and Families," 802, https://pediatrics.aappublications.org/content/pediatrics/early/2011/03/28/peds.2011-0054.full.pdf.

Chapter 3

1. G. E. M, Anscombe, *Intention,* 2nd ed. (Harvard University Press, 1963), 40.

2. This is a topic we will come back to when we size up the prospects for personal meaning in the final chapter of his book.

3. Olivia B. Waxman, " 'We're Still in the Same Boat': As the World Marks 75 Years Since D-Day, the Men Who Were There Look Back—and Ahead," *Time,* June 5, 2019, https://time.com/5595104/d-day-veterans-remember/.

Chapter 4

1. Isabella Poggi, "Enthusiasm and Its Contagion: Nature and Function," in *Affective Computing and Intelligent Interaction,* ed. Ana Paiva, Rui Prada, and Rosalind W. Picard (Springer, 2007), 410–21.

2. Seneca, *On Anger,* Book 2, Paragraph 2, http://www.sophia-project.org/uploads/1/3/9/5/13955288/seneca_anger.pdf.

3. Martha C. Nussbaum, *Anger and Forgiveness: Resentment, Generosity, Justice* (Oxford University Press, 2016), 23.

4. William James, "What Is an Emotion?," *Mind* 9, no. 34 (1884): 188–205.

5. James, 190.

6. Robert Solomon, *The Passions* (Anchor Press/Doubleday, 1977), 150.

7. Frans De Waal, *Mama's Last Hug: Animal Emotions and What They Tell Us about Ourselves* (W.W. Norton & Company, 2019), 126.

8. Poggi, "Enthusiasm and Its Contagion: Nature and Function."

9. David Hume, *A Treatise of Human Nature,* Book III, sect. 1, 8.

Chapter 5

1. There is current philosophical debate about whether relational meaning is the source of individual meaning or individual meaning the source of relational meaning. From our perspective, there is no need to put one before the other. The same imaginative act projected her movement and their movement. The intention she projected in that moment was both hers and theirs, their shared struggle to coordinate that joint achievement. Dan Zahavi discusses this ongoing debate in his essay "We in Me or Me in We? Collective Intentionality and Selfhood," *Journal of Social Ontology* 7, no. 1 (2021): 1–20.

2. "The benefits for children who'd achieved secure attachments accrued as time went on. At age 4.5, they had significantly lower rates of depression and anxiety and fewer 'callous unemotional traits' (limited empathy, lack of

guilt, shallow affect) than their peers still in institutions. About 40 percent of teenagers in the study who'd ever been in orphanages, in fact, were eventually diagnosed with a major psychiatric condition. Their growth was stunted, and their motor skills and language development stalled. MRI studies revealed that the brain volume of the still-institutionalized children was below that of the never institutionalized, and EEGs showed profoundly less brain activity." Melissa Fay Greene, "Decades Ago, Romania Deprived Thousands of Babies of Human Contact," *Atlantic,* July/August 2020, https://www.theatlantic.com/magazine/archive/2020/07/can-an-unloved-child-learn-to-love/612253/.

3. John Stuart Mill, *Utilitarianism in Utilitarianism with Critical Essays,* ed. Samuel Gorovitz (Bobbs-Merrill, 1971), 21.

4. David Hume, *A Treatise of Human Nature,* ed. Ernest C. Mossner (Penguin Books, 1969), 367, 417–18; cf. David Hume, *An Enquiry Concerning the Principles of Morals* (Open Court, 1966), 60; Adam Smith, *An Inquiry into the Nature and Causes of the Wealth of Nations* (Regnery Publishing, 1998, 64; Adam Smith, *The Theory of Moral Sentiments,* ed. D. D. Raphael and A. L. Macfie (Clarendon Press, 1976), 69.

5. In more recent times, a newer word, "empathy," has come to be used for being *with* someone emotionally. "Sympathy" has drifted into meaning a more detached appreciation for another's predicament.

6. John Rawls, *Theory of Justice* (Harvard University Press, 1961), 30–31.

7. Philippa Foot, *Virtues and Vices and Other Essays in Moral Philosophy* (Clarendon Press, 2002), 165, 173.

Chapter 6

1. Paul Tillich, *The Courage to Be* (Yale University Press, 1952), 47.

2. Thaddeus Metz, "The Meaning of Life," in *Stanford Encyclopedia of Philosophy* (Stanford University, 1997–), published May 15, 2007; last modified February 9, 2021, https://plato.stanford.edu/entries/life-meaning/. I have omitted the citations he provides.

3. Harry Frankfurt, *The Reasons of Love* (Princeton University Press, 2014). The quotations in the next two paragraphs come from pp. 64–66.

4. Metz, "The Meaning of Life."

5. Ibid.

6. Ibid.

7. Ibid.

8. Ibid.

9. Ibid.

10. Ibid.

11. Todd May, *A Significant Life: Human Meaning in a Silent Universe* (University of Chicago Press, 2015), 139.

12. Ibid., 22.

13. Ibid., 157.

14. Ibid., 158.

15. Ibid., 156.

16. Susan Wolf, *Meaning in Life and Why It Matters* (Princeton University Press, 2010), 10.

17. Søren Kierkegaard, *Either/Or Part I*, ed. and trans. Howard V. Hong and Edna H. Hong (Princeton University Press, 1987).

Bibliography

American Academy of Pediatrics (2011) "Clinical Report—The Impact of Social Media on Children, Adolescents and Families." https://pediatrics.aappub-lications.org/content/pediatrics/early/2011/03/28/peds.2011-0054.full.pdf.

Anscombe, G. E. M. *Intention*. 2nd ed. Harvard University Press, 1963.

Arendt, Hannah. *The Origins of Totalitarianism*. Harvest, 1968.

Aristotle. *The Basic Works of Aristotle*. Edited and with an introduction by Richard McKeon. Random House, 1941.

Ayer, A. J. *The Meaning of Life*. Charles Scribner's Sons, 1990.

Baars, Bernard. *In the Theater of Consciousness*. Oxford University Press, 1997.

Brewer, Talbot. "The Great Malformation." *Hedgehog Review*, Summer 2023.

Brown, R., and A. Gilman. "The Pronouns of Power and Solidarity." In *Style in Language*, edited by T. A. Sebeok, 253–76. MIT Press, 1960.

Buford, Thomas O. *Trust, Our Second Nature*. Lexington Books, 2009.

Descartes, René. *Meditations on First Philosophy*. Reprinted in "Dreams and Dreaming." In *Stanford Encyclopedia of Philosophy*. Stanford University, 1997–. Article published April 9, 2015. Last modified November 27, 2019. https://plato.stanford.edu/entries/dreams-dreaming/.

Davidson, Donald. *Essays on Actions and Events*. Oxford University Press, 1980.

Deevers, Dusty. "End 'No Fault Divorce.'" *American Reformer*, December 2, 2023. https://americanreformer.org/2023/12/end-no-fault-divorce/.

De Waal, Frans. *Mama's Last Hug: Animal Emotions and What They Tell Us about Ourselves*. W.W Norton & Company, 2019.

Foot, Philippa. *Virtues and Vices and Other Essays in Moral Philosophy*. Clarendon Press, 2002.

Frankfurt, Harry. *The Reasons of Love*. Princeton University Press, 2004.

Friedman, Marilyn. "Friendship and Moral Growth." *Journal of Value Inquiry* 23 (1989): 3–13.

Girard, René. *Things Hidden since the Foundation of the World*. Translated by Stephen Bann and Michael Merteer. Stanford University Press, 1978.

Greene, Melissa Fay. "Decades Ago, Romania Deprived Thousands of Babies of Human Contact." *Atlantic*, July/August 2020. https://www.theatlantic.com/magazine/archive/2020/07/can-an-unloved-child-learn-to-love/612253/.

Hare, R. M. *The Language of Morals*. Clarendon Press, 1952.

Hartland-Swann, John. "The Logic of 'Knowing Jones.'" *Philosophical Studies* 8, no. 1–2 (1957): 1–7.

Haybron, Daniel M. *The Pursuit of Unhappiness: The Elusive Psychology of Well-Being*. Oxford University Press, 2008.

Helm, Bennett. "Friendship." In *Stanford Encyclopedia of Philosophy*. Stanford University, 1997–. Published May 17, 2005; last modified July 30, 2021. https://plato.stanford.edu/entries/friendship/

Hume, David. *A Treatise of Human Nature*. Edited by Ernest C. Mossner. Penguin Books, 1969.

Hume, David. *An Enquiry Concerning the Principles of Morals*. Open Court, 1966.

Hursthouse, Rosalind, and Glen Pettigrove. "Virtue Ethics." In *Stanford Encyclopedia of Philosophy*. Stanford University, 1997–. Published July 18, 2003; last modified October 11, 2022. https://plato.stanford.edu/entries/ethics-virtue/.

Husserl, Edmund. *On the Phenomenology of the Consciousness of Internal Time*. Translated by J. B. Brough. Kluwer, 1990.

James, William. *The Principles of Psychology*. Henry Holt & Company, 1890.

James, William. "What Is an Emotion?" *Mind* 9, no. 34 (1884): 188–205.

Kant, Immanuel. *Groundwork for the Metaphysics of Morals*. Translated by James W. Ellington. Hackett, 1993.

Kant, Immanuel. *The Metaphysical Elements of Justice*. Translated by John Ladd. Prentice-Hall, 1965.

Kant, Immanuel. *Prolegomena to Any Future Metaphysics*. Translated by Lewis White Beck. Bobs-Merrill, 1975.

Kantorowicz, Ernst H. *The King's Two Bodies: A Study in Medieval Political Theology*. Princeton University Press, 1957.

Kierkegaard, Søren. *Either/Or Part I*. Edited and translated by Howard V. Hong and Edna H. Hong. Princeton University Press, 1987.

Krutch, Joseph Wood. *Samuel Johnson*. Henry Holt & Company, 1944.

May, Todd. *A Significant Life: Human Meaning in a Silent Universe*. University of Chicago Press, 2015.

Melden, A. I. *Free Action*. Routledge and Kegan Paul, 1961.

Metz, Thaddeus. "Recent Work on the Meaning of Life." *Ethics* 112, no. 4 (2002): 781–814.

Milgrim, Elijah. "Aristotle on Making Other Selves." *Canadian Journal of Philosophy* 17, no. 2 (1987): 361–76.

Mill, John Stuart. *Utilitarianism in Utilitarianism with Critical Essays*. Edited by Samuel Gorovitz. Bobbs-Merrill, 1971.

Naiman, Rubin. "Dreamless: The Silent Epidemic of REM Sleep Loss." *New York Academy of Sciences* 1406 (2017): 77–85.

Nash, Ronald Alan. "Cognitive Theories of Emotion." *Nous* 23, no. 4 (1989): 481–504.

Neu, Jerome. *A Tear Is an Intellectual Thing.* Oxford University Press, 2000.

Neu, Jerome. *Emotion, Thought, and Therapy.* University of California Press, 1977.

Nozick, Robert. *Philosophical Explanations.* Harvard University Press, 1981.

Nussbaum, Martha C. *Anger and Forgiveness: Resentment, Generosity, Justice.* Oxford University Press, 2016.

O'Brien, Sharon. "The Importance of Dreams." *Clinical Advisor*, December 15, 2016. https://www.clinicaladvisor.com/home/the-waiting-room/the-importance-of-dreams/.

Poggi, Isabella. "Enthusiasm and Its Contagion: Nature and Function." In *Affective Computing and Intelligent Interaction*, edited by Ana Paiva, Rui Prada, and Rosalind W. Picard, 410–21. Springer, 2007.

Parfit, Derek. *Reasons and Persons.* Clarendon Press, 1984.

Prust, Richard, and Jeffery Geller. *Personal Identity in Moral and Legal Reasoning.* Vernon Press, 2019.

Rawls, John. *A Theory of Justice.* Harvard University Press, 1971.

Sebeok, T. A., ed. *Style in Language.* MIT Press, 1960.

Seneca, *On Anger*, Book 2, Paragraph 2. http://www.sophia-project.org/uploads/1/3/9/5/13955288/seneca_anger.pdf.

Smith, Adam. *An Inquiry into the Nature and Causes of the Wealth of Nations.* Regnery Publishing, 1998.

Smith, Adam. *The Theory of Moral Sentiments.* Edited by D. D. Raphael and A. L. Macfie. Clarendon Press, 1976.

Solomon, Robert C. *The Passions.* Anchor Press/Doubleday, 1977.

Solomon, Robert C. "Emotions, Cognition, Affect: On Jerry Neu's 'A Tear is an Intellectual Thing.'" *Philosophical Studies* 108, no. 1/2 (2002): 133–42.

Strawson, Peter. "Freedom and Resentment." *Proceedings of the British Academy 48 (1962):* 1–25.

Stroud, Sarah, and Larisa Svirsky. "Weakness of Will." *In Stanford Encyclopedia of Philosophy.* Stanford University, 1997–. Published May 14, 2008; last modified September 4, 2019. https://plato.stanford.edu/archives/win2021/entries/weakness-will/.

Tillich, Paul. *The Courage to Be.* Yale University Press, 1952.

Velleman, J. D. *The Possibility of Practical Reason.* 2nd ed. Maize Books, 2015.

Wolf, Susan. *Meaning in Life and Why It Matters.* Princeton University Press, 2010.

Zahavi, Dan. "We in Me or Me in We? Collective Intentionality and Selfhood." *Journal of Social Ontology* 7, no. 1 (2021): 1–20.

Index